Many books come with great principles and ideas, but they often lack what Larry Dugger gives in this book. He gives a forty-day plan of action that will strengthen you on your journey through life's wilderness. This book blessed me, and it will bless you.

—Dr. Ron Phillips
Author and Pastor, Abba's House

No book is a fix-all. Rather, a good book such as this one will provide a mirror image and reflect the reader's heart. Throughout the pages of Larry Dugger's debut book, *Forty Days to Defeat Your Past*, I saw my own inconsistencies of character that were holding me back from the true path to reaching the plan God designed for me. I am grateful for Larry's vulnerability and openness as he shares his own struggles while giving practical steps toward the desired change.

—Tracey Bateman
Award-Winning Author of More Than Forty
Novels, Including The Color of the Soul

In his book, *Forty Days to Defeat Your Past*, Larry Dugger accomplishes something that seems to be a struggle for most authors: practicality, relevance, and do-ability. He offers practical teaching from God's Word that is relevant. And he addresses serious issues in a humorous way while laying out a simple plan with doable solutions. When implemented, these solutions will cause the chains from the past to be broken   od's best.

                                                          Landers
F   urch.tv

D1512112

Larry Dugger has an open and engaging writing style that makes for an enjoyable read. The personal anecdotes he relates are interesting and encouraging. His knowledge and understanding of the Scriptures make this book very practical and easy to comprehend. This book offers incredible insights to the believer, as well as anyone who is searching for how to overcome in any area of his life. I have personally taught the concepts in this book to my congregation and have seen incredible results. Larry hit the nail on the head with this excellent book. It is for anyone at any age who struggles with overcoming. I am pleased to recommend this book.

—RANDY COWART
LEAD PASTOR, THE CITY CHURCH, MYCITYCHURCH.TV
AUBURN, ALABAMA

40 days
to defeat *your*
Past

Larry Dugger

40 days to defeat your Past

CHARISMA
HOUSE

Most CHARISMA HOUSE BOOK GROUP products are available at special quantity discounts for bulk purchase for sales promotions, premiums, fund-raising, and educational needs. For details, write Charisma House Book Group, 600 Rinehart Road, Lake Mary, Florida 32746, or telephone (407) 333-0600.

FORTY DAYS TO DEFEAT YOUR PAST by Larry Dugger
Published by Charisma House
Charisma Media/Charisma House Book Group
600 Rinehart Road
Lake Mary, Florida 32746
www.charismahouse.com

Unless otherwise noted, all Scripture quotations are taken from the Holy Bible, Modern English Version. Copyright © 2014 by Military Bible Association. Used by permission. All rights reserved.

Scripture quotations marked KJV are from the King James Version of the Bible.

Library of Congress Cataloging-in-Publication Data:
Names: Dugger, Larry, author.
Title: Forty days to defeat your past / Larry Dugger.
Description: Lake Mary, Florida : Charisma House,
[2016] | Includes
   bibliographical references and index.
Identifiers: LCCN 2016006580| ISBN 9781629986951
(trade paper : alk. paper) |
   ISBN 9781629986968 (e-book : alk. paper)
Subjects: LCSH: Habit breaking--Religious aspects--
Christianity. |
   Success--Religious aspects--Christianity.
Classification: LCC BV4598.7 .D84 2016 | DDC
248.4--dc23
LC record available at http://lccn.loc.gov/2016006580

While the author has made every effort to provide
accurate Internet addresses at the time of publication,
neither the publisher nor the author assumes any
responsibility for errors or for changes that occur after
publication.

First edition

16 17 18 19 20 — 987654321
Printed in the United States of America

To Jesus

Because You faced the Devil for forty days, now I can face mine.

CONTENTS

Part III
Don't Try to Save What
God's Trying to Drown

Part IV
It's Just the Usual

Part V
Defiance on a Daily Basis

Part VI
Mission: Impossible

Part VII
Don't Just Dream While You Are Asleep

Part VIII
Want to Trade?

Part IX
Cut the Bull and Make the Sacrifice

Part X
Change Is Possible When You Have Had Enough

Part XI
Mummy-Making Is Serious Business

Part XII
The Most Dangerous Place Is "Almost There"

ACKNOWLEDGMENTS

I WOULD LIKE TO express my sincere gratitude:

To My wife, Karen, and our two sons, Trent and Payte. Thank you for your unwavering support and encouragement. The long evenings and weekends spent writing required family sacrifice and the occasional change in plans. Your understanding and backing kept me focused as the weeks turned into months.

To the congregation of Real Life Church. You were the first to hear this message. The transformation I witnessed in the lives of so many of you became my inspiration for writing this book. The obvious change that was taking place in your lives kept me going during those long days of writing and editing. We took this journey together, and now we are no longer the same.

To Tracey Bateman, my mentor and writing coach. Thank you for pushing me past my usual limitations and helping to stir up the gifts within me. Your wisdom and guidance directed me as I worked to bring these pages together. You are not only a gifted writer but also an anointed teacher.

Finally to my parents, Larry and Lisa Dugger. Thank you for teaching me the importance of hard work and demonstrating how life can turn around when you decide to face your devils.

INTRODUCTION

IS SOMETHING KEEPING you from the life you've always dreamed of? Do you struggle with an addiction or bad habit that you just can't seem to break? Have you tried to change again and again only to end up back in the same old cycle of behavior that leaves you exactly where you don't want to be? There is a way to gain victory over those battles—to unbecome everything you were never meant to be and rediscover the person you were before the struggles of life happened to you. But becoming who you really are will require you to take a different path, to pursue another way of living. If you will journey with me over the next forty days, I will show you the way.

The number forty has deep spiritual significance. Over and over in Scripture we see the number forty connected to new beginnings, being released from prison, victory over opponents, and the ability to win battles you usually lose. When God wanted to bring transformation, often the process lasted forty days.

It rained forty days and forty nights after Noah built the ark, then he and his family remained in the ark another forty days while the water receded. When they finally exited the boat, the world around them was different, new. They stepped off the ark and into a new start.

Goliath, the giant of Gath, taunted Israel's army morning

and evening for forty days. It became like clockwork. But then a young shepherd boy rose up and refused to listen to his insults any longer. After that epic showdown David was no longer viewed as just a shepherd boy; he was now a mighty warrior and would eventually become Israel's next king.

Most importantly Jesus faced off with the Devil for forty days in the wilderness. By not giving in to the enemy's temptations, Jesus was able to fulfill His purpose, which was to secure the salvation of mankind through His death on the cross. That would not have been possible had Jesus succumbed to sin.

But something else happened in that wilderness. The Bible says Jesus went into the wilderness "full of the Holy Spirit" (Luke 4:1, NIV). Yet when He left, He "returned in the power of the Spirit to Galilee. And His fame went throughout the surrounding region" (Luke 4:14). After standing up to the Devil, Jesus began to walk in a level of power and authority that He hadn't demonstrated up to that point.

Forty days can mark the beginning of your transformation too. It can be the starting point that leads you to the life you've only dreamed about.

Before we go any further, I want to make a note about the term *devil*. In this book I make a distinction between the figure in Scripture and the behavior we often pin on him. For the purpose of this teaching, the biblical character is capitalized while the behavior he sometimes represents will be lowercased. For example: The Devil wants you to believe you have no power over your devils.

It's Time to Square Off
With Your Devils

If we want a life of freedom and victory, we must square off with our devils, just as Jesus squared off with the Devil in the wilderness. The devils I'm referring to are the old, familiar patterns of behavior that keep us experiencing the same unwanted results.

Sometimes when we seek change, we say, "I can never become the person I want to be." But maybe the journey isn't always about becoming something new. Maybe it's about turning from what you've become so you can be who you really are.

The person you currently are was shaped by the past. While that may sound like bad news, the good news is what you do right now will decide who you become in the future. You can become great!

I must be candid with you. At times writing this book was very difficult. The amount of spiritual warfare that bombarded each keystroke often left me overwhelmed. I was required to open my heart and share my personal devils with you, and like you, I am not proud of my struggles.

Like you, I am human. I bleed when others cut me, and I occasionally miss the mark. I felt under-qualified when the Holy Spirit tapped my shoulder and asked me to write this book. I had no idea what I was getting into or that the Devil would take it so personally.

I wrote this book for you. As the days turned into weeks and the weeks into months, I found myself in a perpetual loop of desperation. I begged God to help you. Daily I found myself crying out on your behalf. I asked God to give you what you needed to put the devils you face under your feet once and for all. I may not know you personally, but I have fought for you. Jesus also fought for you. Now it's your turn to fight for yourself. You're worth it!

If you'll choose to square off with your devils, this book will take you step-by-step through a forty-day process that will help you identify and defeat the destructive patterns that so often leave you flat on your face. Each day of this journey offers a unique perspective on what the devil wreaking havoc in your life is scheming. Here is what you can expect:

* A daily motivation—This will help you discern what the devil is up to at any given point in your forty-day journey. It offers both a warning and an encouragement. I suggest you read this and the rest of the day's entry first thing in the morning so you will already be aware of the enemy's battle plan.

* A key verse—The verse will always be tied to whatever the goal is for that particular day. If you have trouble remembering Scripture, I suggest you write down the verse on index cards and place them in key locations where you will be sure to see them as you move through your day.

* A reflection journal—At the end of each day you will be asked a question or series of questions.

These are designed to help you better understand how your devil has been sabotaging your
life. Even if the answer is painful and hard to
accept, honesty is of the utmost importance. You
cannot change what you will not own. Space has
been provided for you to journal. Journaling has
many benefits. Spend some time reflecting on how
the day went. If you had a bad day, write about
it. Don't be afraid to open up and bleed on the
pages. God can handle your honesty. Think about
the question posed at the end of each day and get
laser focused as you journal.

Laced throughout this book are the real stories of fellow
strugglers who faced their devils. After writing the mate-
rial you are about to read, I traveled across the country and
tested this concept on regular, everyday Christ followers.
The results were nothing short of amazing! You will see
how ordinary people overcame giant-size devils and in the
process rediscovered the person they thought they had lost
forever. You will be encouraged by their transformation.

You know it's time for a change. If you'll follow this road
map to victory, "The God of peace will soon crush Satan
under your feet" (Rom. 16:20).

That's not an empty promise. I speak from personal experience. I know what it is like to feel the power of temptation.
I know what it's like to have a past that is always in hot pursuit. I am constantly reminded that my flesh is fighting for
control, but I also realize that my future doesn't have to be
dictated by my past. It depends upon my current choices.

FINDING THE WAY BACK

When I was in Bible college, we were never taught that after twenty years of ministry it would still be a daily struggle to maintain purity, forgive those who treated us unfairly, and let go of the devils from our past. I was fighting all three battles the day the idea for this book came to me. I was sitting in my office reading Luke chapter 4 as my daily Bible reading.

I had been fighting some personal battles for a long time and was beginning to get very discouraged. For the first time in my life I really thought I might not make it. This time the battle seemed different. The Devil seemed to have the upper hand, and he knew it.

I felt like the Apostle Paul who said, "The right things that I want to do, I never seem to be able to do, and the wrong things that I said I would never do again, I end up doing." (See Romans 7:15–20.) The desire I had for change and my ability to make it happen seemed a million miles apart. I placed my head on my desk and silently begged God for help.

At this point my résumé was a lot more impressive than my life. My résumé said, "Pastor, professional counselor, giant killer, and superhero!" My life said something very different. I was questioning everything: the ministry, my marriage, and the future. My flesh was staging a revolt. I felt as if my life was scattered like the pieces of a puzzle, and I wasn't sure how or if I could put them back together. I knew that if I was to overcome, I would have to confront myself, my thoughts, and my feelings.

Would I ever find my way back?

Like Jesus, I was being tempted in my areas of weakness. The snake was whispering, "Go ahead." I had a choice to make. Listen to the snake, reach out and take what is desirable, or face the snake and find the future the Devil was trying to take from me. Either way, I would be required to confront the Devil. I could face him or I could give in to him. The choice was mine.

As I read through Luke 4:1–13, where Satan tempted Jesus in the wilderness, the answer suddenly became so clear to me. This man, Jesus, who had lived two thousand years ago, was just like me. He fought the same devils that I do. For the first time in my life I realized just how human Jesus was. I began to understand that the reason Jesus was successful was because He chose to face the Devil.

Even though I had read that story on multiple occasions, I had overlooked the fact that Jesus was not just battling the Devil. He was also battling Himself. Spiritual maturity doesn't take you out of the fight.

Sure my devils are different than Jesus's were, but the fact remains: I must face them. Like Jesus, I would have to spend some time in the wilderness facing what stood in opposition to my future. I quickly realized that I had to confront those things in myself that threatened to keep me from who I wanted to be. That was the day my life changed.

If Jesus could do it, Larry could do it too—and so can you!

Before any battle can be won, the soldier must decide to show up for the fight. Jesus showed up in the wilderness to fight the Devil. Will you show up to fight yours?

CHOOSE TO SHOW UP

Jesus, being filled with the Holy Spirit, returned from the Jordan and was led by the Spirit into the wilderness, being tempted by the devil for forty days. During those days He ate nothing. And when they were ended, He was hungry.

—LUKE 4:1–2

Jesus went into the wilderness to prepare for ministry and eventually death. But before He ever stretched out His hand in healing or met the woman at the well, before the whip would tear through His back exposing muscle and bone, before the nails would split the tendons in His wrists, before the thorns would poke holes in God's Son, much preparation was needed. However, as Jesus faced the Devil in preparation for His eventual death, something wonderful happened.

Suddenly He was prepared for life! Those forty days weren't about the Devil at all. They were about Him! During His forty days, there were no friends cheering Him on. There was no polished praise band to electrify the atmosphere. No small groups to hold His hand. Just Jesus and the Devil engaged in an epic battle that would forever decide His future and yours and mine.

During this forty-day challenge you are going to have to show up. No one could win the battle for Jesus, and no one can do it for you. When you decide to confront yourself by spending forty days in a face-off with your devils, it will get lonely, but remember, you're not alone. Jesus has already been there. Follow the footsteps in the sand.

If you don't go all the way with me, through thick and thin, you don't deserve me. If your first concern is to look at yourself, you'll never find yourself. But if you forget about yourself and look to me, you'll find both yourself and me.

—MATTHEW 10:38–39, THE MESSAGE

These are powerful words. They were spoken by a man who knew exactly what it would take to reach His destiny. He knows there is a certain amount of dying necessary if you want to truly live. Jesus essentially said in Matthew 10, "When life is all about you, you will never find yourself." He understood what it meant to show up in the wilderness, push past His comfort zones, confront His humanity, and face the Devil.

If you're like me, you've no doubt spent your fair share of time with the enemy. You also probably realize the only real power the Devil has in your life is the power that you give him. He desperately wants you to believe there are certain things you have no power to change. He wants you to settle for a life that is far less than God's plan. Jesus had many encounters with the Devil and one of those encounters is going to set the stage for the next forty days of your life. Keep in mind that Jesus was a human being just like you.

When Jesus came to the earth as Mary's baby, He laid aside His deity and became a living, breathing human. Jesus lived in a body just like yours. Think about it. Jesus knows what you go through! For me, it's a great source of comfort to know that Jesus's stomach growled when He was hungry, that His face turned red and maybe got a little hot when His enemies cursed Him and friends betrayed

Him. As a popular, charismatic man of His day, I am sure women were always trying to entice Him to lay down His purity. When women are washing your feet with their tears, you'd better be a disciplined man.

Jesus was real. He had family problems, friend problems, cultural problems, church problems. Jesus was a lot more like you and me than you may think. It is important that you understand just how human Jesus was. He was in all points tempted as we are, yet He was without sin (Heb. 4:15). For Jesus to really be able to help us, He had to become one of us. That means He fought battles that are familiar to us!

Jesus was God wrapped in flesh; we are flesh wrapped in God. However you describe it, flesh always fights for control. Jesus was not exempt.

Jesus, being filled with the Holy Spirit, returned from the Jordan and was led by the Spirit into the wilderness, being tempted by the devil for forty days. During those days He ate nothing. And when they were ended, He was hungry.

The devil said to Him, "If You are the Son of God, command this stone to become bread."

Jesus answered him, "It is written, 'Man shall not live by bread alone, but by every word of God.'"

The devil, taking Him up onto a high mountain, showed Him all the kingdoms of the world in a moment of time. And the devil said to Him, "I will give You all this power and their glory, for it has been delivered to me. And I give it to whomever I will. If You, then, will worship me, all will be Yours."

And Jesus answered him, "Get behind Me, Satan! For it is written, 'You shall worship the Lord your God, and Him only shall you serve.'" He brought Him to Jerusalem, set Him on the pinnacle of the temple, and said to Him, "If You are the Son of God, throw Yourself down from here. For it is written: 'He shall give His angels charge concerning you, to preserve you,' and 'In their hands they shall hold you up, lest you strike your foot against a stone.'" Jesus answered him, "It is said, 'You shall not tempt the Lord your God.'" When the devil had ended all the temptations, he departed from Him until another time.

—Luke 4:1–13

Jesus faced His forty-day challenge. Will you?

When Jesus was crucifying His flesh and beating His body into subjection, the Devil was right there to try and stop Him from achieving results. The Devil was walking beside Him step for step. If you're waiting until there is no opposition to face your opponents and bring discipline into your life, it is never going to happen.

You must stand toe-to-toe with your opposition.

You can always find an excuse not to take charge of your life, but the key to success is to do what is necessary despite the opposition.

Keep in mind that even Jesus had to face His opposition. God would not deliver Him from it, but He did empower Him for victory. God has also empowered *you*. The Bible says, "He who is in you is greater than he who is in the world" (1 John 4:4).

IDENTIFY YOUR CAUSE

We don't know a lot about the first thirty years of the life of Jesus. We start getting details of His life after He is an adult. As Jesus approached thirty years of age, He identified His cause, chose His team, and started working to accomplish His goals.

The first step in this forty-day challenge is being willing to confront yourself and identify the things that hold you back. Those things will become your cause and the focus of your attention for the next forty days.

Do you struggle with losing weight, breaking a negative habit, offering forgiveness, releasing bitterness, cleaning up your thought life, overcoming an addiction, getting past trauma from your childhood, family dysfunction, or marriage problems? Or maybe you struggle with something such as being a procrastinator, cleaning your house, being uptight all the time, balancing your checkbook, or never being able to keep your commitments.

Whatever your opposition, it is important that you take this time to identify exactly what holds you back. You cannot change what you will not acknowledge as being a problem. This is not a self-help book but rather a self-confrontation book. You have been helping yourself for far too long. It is time to confront the person you have become.

The principles of this book will impact you only if you're willing to be completely honest about your devils. I found it very difficult to be honest with myself about the condition of my life. It is always easier to point out the flaws and character defects in others rather than being honest about the condition of your own heart.

Take a few minutes to think about what your cause is going to be and write down what you would like to gain victory over during your forty-day challenge.

My cause is:

_____

_____

_____

Before Jesus could get His breakthrough and move on to His intended future, He was required to spend forty days in the wilderness facing His greatest opponent, the Devil. You have already identified your greatest opponent and now it's time for you, like Jesus, to carve out forty days of your life to establish the future God has for you.

During this forty-day challenge, we are going to work to establish a new "normal" pattern. It will require tenacity and determination, but if you are willing to set your mind and heart on achieving your goals, it can happen.

Since you've identified your cause, now decide when you will begin.

My forty-day journey begins on:

_____

_____

_____

Remember, don't wait until you have reached your goal to be proud of yourself. Be proud of each step you take along the way.

Now that you have identified your cause and selected a starting date, you are ready to begin. But first I would like to pray for you.

> *Heavenly Father, I ask for Your help. Old enemies are anticipating an attack. Even now familiar devils are wringing their hands in excitement as they wait for us to engage them on the battlefield. This time let the battle end differently. Like Jesus, keep us focused and moving forward. Help us to be as ferocious in attacking our devils as they have been in attacking us. When the enemy begs for mercy, may he find none. In Jesus's name, amen.*

PART I

THE DEVIL WANTS YOU TO TRADE GROWTH FOR GRATIFICATION

We must accept all of God's will for us, not just those portions that happen to appeal and bring instant gratification and pleasure to us.[1]

—ROD PARSLEY

Day 1

CHURCH CLOTHES CAN
HIDE ONLY SO MUCH

There are two places where we usually portray a life that
is far different from the one we actually live: church
and Facebook. Today expect your hiding places to be
challenged. Unlike Adam, don't be afraid to confront
your nakedness. Choose growth over gratification.

Key Verse: *He said, "I heard Your voice in the garden
and was afraid because I was naked, so I hid myself.*
—GENESIS 3:10

A S HAPPENED TO Adam and his wife, Eve, life can leave
us hiding naked behind the trees, afraid and regretting
past decisions. Once mankind was placed in Eden, it didn't
take long for the Devil to make his first appearance. He
came with an offer, and Adam and Eve did what we usually
do—they chose to satisfy the selfish desires of their flesh
rather than grow into the champion God created them to be.

The rogue ex-archangel was successful in his attempt to
get mankind off the track God intended for them. Adam
and Eve ate the forbidden and traded God's glory for a
life of fig leaves. Then they played a game of hide-and-seek
with God.

Then they heard the sound of the LORD God walking in
the garden in the cool of the day, and the man and his

wife hid themselves from the presence of the Lord God
among the trees of the garden.

—Genesis 3:8

Does that sound familiar? The church has always been
a place for professional hiders. We hide behind our titles,
neckties, and twenty-pound study Bibles instead of being
real about our nakedness.

Sometimes we look at other Christians, especially those
on television, and all we see are perfect people living perfect lives without any real problems. They're driving new
cars, living in beautiful homes, flashing perfect smiles, and
sporting the latest in fashion. That, however, is not the
reality. In reality most people are hurting, fighting, and
losing the same battles over and over again. We're struggling with bad habits, and making and breaking promises
to ourselves on a daily basis. That, my friends, is how it is
in the real world.

Over the last two decades I have had many titles:
pastor, counselor, husband, father, son, brother, and friend.
Through each of those roles, I have been made painfully
aware that those of us who are supposed to have it all
together can sometimes be secretly falling apart.

There have even been times when the nameplate on my
door should have said "pretender" rather than "pastor." Can
you relate?

We go to church on Sunday and sing "I Surrender All,"
only to return home and change our tune to "I Surrender
Some." The future gets lost in our battle with the past. The
good news is, it doesn't have to be that way.

The Lord God called to the man and said to him, "Where are you?"

—Genesis 3:9

God was not requesting Adam's physical location. Obviously God knew his hiding spot. God was more interested in Adam's spiritual location. Despite what Adam had done, God was still looking for him. Adam's future was not lost. Yes, he had given in to the voice of gratification. However, God would give him another chance.

When you think about the future, what comes to your mind? Do you suddenly feel worry, dread, or even panic? Do you think about the obstacles that always seem to be in your way? As Adam did, do you have a favorite hiding spot?

Perhaps your mind goes to behaviors and habits you know need to change but that you continue to struggle with year after year. You stay trapped in the patterns of the past. Gratification always seems to trump growth. If this is where you find yourself year after year, I must ask, what do you truly believe about your future?

God is thinking about your future, and His vision for you is good. He said:

For I know the plans I have for you…plans to prosper you and not to harm you, plans to give you hope and a future.

—Jeremiah 29:11, niv

Your future is waiting just beyond your willingness to confront yourself and, as Jesus did, face the Devil.

Your future can be discovered or it can be lost. It is not

defined by your past, family, failure, or even the Devil. It is defined by you. Your willingness to either conquer or conform to your devils will be the deciding factor. Regardless of what has obstructed you in the past, your future must be constructed—and it must be constructed by you.

Adam would eventually show himself, and God would cover his nakedness. God stands ready to cover your nakedness as well. The life you thought you could never have is closer than you think. Today is the first day of the rest of your life. Welcome to the fight!

REFLECTION JOURNAL

Where does God usually find you hiding? Are you ready to take the mask off and reveal your spiritual location?

_____

_____

_____

_____

_____

_____

_____

_____

_____

_____

Day 2

NEVER TRUST A TALKING SNAKE

Today you can expect the snake to start whispering.
It will be subtle but deliberate. Keep in mind that
he isn't interested in a friendly chat. His objective
is to trick you into cancelling the future you seek.
As Jesus did, refuse to trust a talking snake.

Key Verse: *And Jesus answered him, "Get behind
Me, Satan! For it is written, 'You shall worship the
Lord your God, and Him only shall you serve.'"*

—LUKE 4:8

THE DEVIL YOU face is very talkative. Like my five-year-old
nephew who simply refuses to be quiet, the Devil always
has something to say. Sometimes he speaks through other
people, our flesh, bad habits, or past circumstances. The point
is, he is always talking, and his conversation starters usually
consist of the things that would sabotage our lives and keep
us trapped in the ordinary.

After God created Adam and Eve and placed them in
Eden, it wasn't long before the devil struck up a conversation with Eve.

Now the serpent was more subtle than any beast of the
field which the LORD God had made. And he said to the

21

woman, "Has God said, 'You shall not eat of any tree of
the garden'?"

—GENESIS 3:1

The conversation would prove fatal. Adam and Eve
would go from being caretakers of a beautiful garden to
having to eke out a living from the earth. And once they
were banished from Eden the devil would accompany them,
both the literal Devil and, perhaps to a larger degree, the
behaviors that resulted from their sin.

The Devil always shows up just to chat, at least at first.
Before Eve lost everything, all she did was have a chat with
a snake. Eve listened to him without any kind of resistance.
She chose to take the Devil at his word. As a result, the
quality of her life was greatly diminished.

The Devil would later choose another target, but this
time he would not be so lucky and the outcome would be
far different. His target was God's Son, whom he tempted
for forty days in the wilderness (Luke 4:1–13). But the chat
did not go as planned. That's because after the Devil started
the conversation, Jesus initiated a confrontation.

You too must confront what the Devil is saying to you.
When the Devil starts talking, you decide whether to challenge what he is saying to you. Eve did not do this, and as
a result her life was far less than what it could have been.
Jesus did this, and as a result He went on to fulfill His purpose, which was to save us all.

When the Devil starts speaking to you about your habits,
the past, or the way you have always been, you must choose
to confront whatever he is telling you. Every time the Devil

threw a punch at Jesus, Jesus threw a counter punch. Jesus is your guide. By looking closely at how He handled the Devil, you can learn how to handle your devils.

After the conversation has been initiated and the confrontation has been engaged, there are only two possible outcomes. Either you will conform and, like Eve, accept what the Devil is saying, or you will conquer and, like Jesus, assert complete dominance. The power is yours. You can choose to conform or you can choose to conquer. Your choice will determine the quality of your future.

Jesus understood that conforming to what the Devil was saying was not the answer. Even though it might have been easier at the time, it would not have been to His benefit. What the Devil was offering to Him was convenient, cheap, and easy. But Jesus was looking for more! He conquered because He knew the harder road would lead to the future He longed for.

What about you? Are you looking for more? Are you ready to take the tougher path to move past the place life always seems to leave you?

Let's go back to the day I sat with my head on my desk and my fist clinched in fear. That day I was about to throw away every blessing God had given me. Without God's muscle behind me, I would have definitely turned my back on my dream of being a faithful minister and a godly husband and father, and instead accepted the kingdoms of the world. That day I had to get real about my devils and honest about my inability to face them alone.

I am not going to tell you that this confrontation will be

easy, because it won't be. I will, however, tell you that it will
be worth it.

The Devil is very convincing. He will carefully craft an
argument as to why you should listen to him. Eve fell in to
this trap. The Devil was saying everything she wanted to hear.
The only thing he did not mention were the consequence of
their actions. Why? The devastation of the consequences
would far exceed the excitement of the immediate benefit.

No matter what your past holds, keep in mind that the
future is clean. Life has a reset button; it's called tomorrow.
Just as you can count on the sun coming up in the morning,
you can count on tomorrow being brand new. Your future
will be what you make it!

REFLECTION JOURNAL

Are you prepared to confront what the snake is offering you?
What will you do differently this time? Explain.

_____

_____

_____

_____

_____

_____

_____

_____

_____

Day 3

DO YOU CRAVE GROWTH
OR GRATIFICATION?

By now your cravings are, no doubt, crying
out for gratification. Don't be surprised when
those old, familiar habits occasionally tap your
shoulder. Today focus on the benefit of saying no
rather than the payoff of saying yes to them.

Key Verse: *The devil said to Him, "If You are the Son of
God, command this stone to become bread." Jesus answered
him, "It is written, 'Man shall not live by bread alone.'"*

—LUKE 4:3–4

YOU ALWAYS HAVE two choices. You can give in to the
normal—have a cigarette, eat too much chocolate,
watch the porn, stay home instead of keeping your commitments, give in to insecurity, do what you have always done,
and stay the same. Or you can grow past the point of failure
and experience the life you've always dreamed possible. The
question is, do you crave growth more than you crave gratification? Your answer to that question is critical, because
you will not experience victory over your struggles if you're
always indulging yourself in those areas.

Salvation isn't just about getting man into heaven. It's also
about getting heaven into man so he can live a victorious life.

For me, it is a constant battle to stay at a healthy weight,
so every day I have a decision to make: Do I grow healthier

by making good lifestyle choices or do I gratify myself and
head for IHOP? (You gotta love the Rooty Tooty Fresh
'N Fruity pancake stack!) Do I hit the gym or do I hit the
couch? The power is mine. Will I grow healthier today or
will I give in to the voice of gratification?

Gratification is always calling out to us. Our flesh groans
for the very things that would keep us in bondage. This is
the struggle the Apostle Paul wrote about in his letter to
the Galatians:

> It is obvious what kind of life develops out of trying to
> get your own way all the time: repetitive, loveless, cheap
> sex; a stinking accumulation of mental and emotional
> garbage; frenzied and joyless grabs for happiness; trinket
> gods; magic-show religion; paranoid loneliness; cutthroat
> competition; all-consuming-yet-never-satisfying wants; a
> brutal temper; an impotence to love or be loved; divided
> homes and divided lives; small-minded and lopsided pur-
> suits; the vicious habit of depersonalizing everyone into
> a rival; uncontrolled and uncontrollable addictions; ugly
> parodies of community. I could go on.
>
> —GALATIANS 5:19–21, THE MESSAGE

This is the voice of gratification. Each time it calls, I get
to choose whether or not to answer, and so do you.

I can so understand why the Devil first tempted Jesus
with food in Luke 4. Jesus was starving! He'd literally had
no food for forty days, and by the time Satan confronted
Him, Jesus was more than hungry; He was ravenous! But
the temptation here was much deeper than just turning

stones into bread. The temptation was to get Jesus to listen to the voice of gratification.

The Devil said, "If you are the Son of God, tell this stone to become bread" (Luke 4:3, NIV). The Devil was offering Jesus a power trip. He was saying, "You're hungry. You're the Son of God. Come on, have a little bread."

Jesus could have gotten away with it if He didn't want to fulfill His destiny, but often the problem becomes the fact that the things we can get away *with* today we can't get away *from* tomorrow. For Jesus, the wilderness was about more than facing temptation. It was a test to see if He had what it took to be the pure sacrifice for our sins.

Some of you are using your forty days to lose weight, and you are going to be tempted to turn stones into bread—or better yet, bran into brownies! No doubt some of you are using this time to focus on kicking a habit, such as smoking cigarettes or drinking too much alcohol, and you are going to be tempted to give in and gratify that craving.

During this process you are going to come to a crossroads where you'll face the question: Am I going to indulge my flesh, or am I going to grow past my usual tendencies?

There is a huge difference between growth and gratification, and the difference reveals the more excellent way. Growth is the process of becoming mature. It takes work. Gratification takes no effort whatsoever.

As Albert Einstein is often credited with saying, the definition of insanity is doing the same thing over and over and expecting different results.

Here is the interesting part. Later on in Jesus's ministry

He would multiply loaves of bread on at least two occasions. (See Matthew 14:13–21; 15:32–38.)

It wasn't a sin for Jesus to turn rocks into bread. It was a test to see if He could be moved away from His focus, which was fasting. Not everything that tempts you is necessarily a sin. It might just be an effort to move you away from your focus. For instance, it's not a sin to have fried chicken instead of grilled chicken, but when your focus is to lose weight, fried chicken can get you way off course. It's not a sin to be ten minutes late or to postpone an appointment just because you don't feel like going, but if you're trying to be more studious with your time or more dependable, those things can really hinder you.

Notice with me that when Satan tempted Jesus in Luke 4, he was just making suggestions. He suggested, "You know Jesus, You could if You wanted to." Do you recognize that voice? It's that little voice that says, "You don't have to deprive yourself. You don't have to suffer through these cravings, because you could do this if you wanted to."

We all recognize that voice. It is the voice of gratification. Yes, of course Jesus could have turned rocks into bread if He wanted to—He could have turned Satan into a hot fudge sundae with extra sprinkles if He had wanted to. (That's what I would have done.) But that would have diverted His path. The future was more important to Jesus than instant gratification.

You too are going to have to decide not to do some of the things you want to—"for the flesh desires what is contrary to the Spirit, and the Spirit what is contrary to the flesh.

They are in conflict with each other, so that you are not to do whatever you want" (Gal. 5:17, NIV).

Would Jesus be moved off task? That is what the first temptation was all about. Now that you have made it to day 3, be determined to want what you have never had more than you want what Satan is offering you.

REFLECTION JOURNAL

Do you have weaknesses in your life that aren't necessarily sins but still inhibit your growth? Identify them and explain why you want to change them.

_____

_____

_____

_____

_____

_____

_____

_____

_____

_____

_____

_____

_____

Day 4

THERE ARE NO SHORTCUTS TO SUCCESS

As you move closer to your goal, don't be surprised when the Devil starts pointing out every reason you cannot achieve it. Instead of listening to that chatter, use today to focus on what you can do to change your life and refuse to make others the source of your failure.

Key Verse: *Don't look for shortcuts to God. The market is flooded with surefire, easygoing formulas for a successful life that can be practiced in your spare time. Don't fall for that stuff, even though crowds of people do. The way to life—to God!—is vigorous and requires total attention.*
—MATTHEW 7:13, THE MESSAGE

THE DEVIL WILL always tempt you with shortcuts. I will admit that I am a typical male driver. I am usually on the lookout for a faster route. The problem, however, is that my shortcuts usually end up taking just as long or longer as the original path. Even worse, sometimes they cause me to get lost. My wife says, "Stick to the route, and we will get there safely." I say, "There has to be a faster way!" Sometimes I'm right about that; sometimes I'm wrong. But one thing I have learned for sure: in life there are no shortcuts to success.

The Devil says, "Take the easy way!" Of course he doesn't usually put it quite that way. It typically sounds something like this: "You don't have to finish reading this book. This whole thing about bringing discipline, order, and focus into your life isn't really your style." Or "Diet? No way. That is why they make those stretchy pants!" Or "You have never been an organized person. You have never won that battle in the past. This is just the way you are, and you need to accept it."

You are never going to get where you want to be by taking shortcuts. Doing the work brings success.

In Luke 4 the devil tried to get Jesus to take a shortcut. He took Jesus to Jerusalem and set Him on the pinnacle of the temple. "'If you are the Son of God,' he said, 'throw yourself down from here. For it is written: "He will command his angels concerning you to guard you carefully; they will lift you up in their hands, so that you will not strike your foot against a stone."' Jesus answered, 'It is said: "Do not put the Lord your God to the test"'" (Luke 4:9–12, NIV).

A shortcut is an all-out effort by the Devil to remove you from personal responsibility. In Luke 4 the Devil was basically telling Jesus, "Let the angels worry about it." He was saying, "Let the angels catch You; it's their responsibility."

When you refuse to take responsibility for your own life, you will always be jumping off a cliff and hoping someone else catches you. Better yet, when you do jump off a cliff and splatter on the rocks below, you will blame those who did not catch you or those you believe pushed you. In your mind it will always be someone else's fault.

Jesus refused to fall into that trap because He knew He was responsible for Himself. His objective was clear: stick to the plan and create the discipline He would later need to face the cross. Jesus was responsible for the sins of the entire human race. His journey to the cross started in that place— with His decision to take full responsibility for His actions.

As things begin to get uncomfortable, you may be tempted to point the finger at someone else and make excuses for your behavior. It's always easier to blame others and say, "They're the reason I am the way I am" rather than, "I am the way that I am because I refuse to take responsibility for myself."

For you to achieve your best, at some point you must own your actions. You have to say, "Hey, that's me never following through on my commitments. That's me doing all those drugs. That's me lying in bed for days because I am too depressed to get up. That's me putting all those unhealthy foods in my body. That's me feeling sorry for myself all the time. That's me thinking all of those terrible thoughts. That's me refusing to forgive and release bitterness."

It's me! It's not the Devil. It's not those circumstances from my past that caused me so much pain. It's not other people. It's me. I am the one not taking ownership of my life. I am the one not taking personal responsibility for myself.

The remainder of this forty-day challenge will be a waste of your time if you are unwilling to recognize and own your contribution to the problem.

Jesus was not about to jump off a building and hope someone else would catch Him. It is impossible to be selfless and irresponsible at the same time. Jesus knew His future depended upon Him and God, and He was not about to give that power away to anyone else, not even the angels.

Jesus was doing more than just thinking about Himself; He was thinking about the future. He was thinking about the countless lives that would be impacted by His decisions.

I realize that sometimes life hands us very difficult situations, and I also realize the power of addiction and depression are very strong. However, the resolve to take responsibility for yourself far exceeds the tragedies of your past and the uncertainties of your present. If you make it out of the wilderness as Jesus did, it will be because you decided to do so.

REFLECTION JOURNAL

Which of your devils have you decided are someone else's responsibility? Are you prepared to shift the focus back to God and yourself?

_____

_____

_____

_____

_____

_____

_____

_____

_____

_____

Real People, Real Stories

Tom's Story

Tom has a story that is all too common. As he sat across from me in Starbucks, I could sense his discomfort. He was embarrassed and ashamed. "I have a serious devil, Larry," he said.

Tom, a deacon and charismatic leader in his church, was addicted to pornography. And he wanted to use the forty-day challenge to confront this hidden monster in his closet.

As we sat together sipping coffee, he explained that pornography had always been a part of his adult life and that he used it as a way to escape thoughts of being rejected by women. "I became addicted before becoming a Christian," he said. "I soon found out that my addiction would follow me into my newfound relationship with Christ."

Even though Tom identified himself as a follower of Christ, there were many occasions when his life didn't look like the Christ he claimed to represent. Tom spent the majority of his free time either in strip clubs, visiting prostitutes, or looking at pornographic websites. Tom was living a double life.

When Tom began his forty-day challenge, his mindset was to take it one day at a time. He said he quickly began to think of his addiction as an enemy rather than as a familiar friend. He now realizes that you don't just face your devil once. No, the monster keeps coming back and you must chose to get in the fight every day.

After completing the forty days, he said, "I learned that just because my forty-day challenge is over, that doesn't mean that my addiction is over. I started looking at my forty days as the training that I would use to guide me for the rest of my life instead of seeing them as something I needed to get through so I could go back to my addiction approach."

Tom is aware that this is a temptation he will have to choose to fight every day, and he has learned that the difference between who you are and who you want to be is what you do. Listen to Tom in his own words as he describes how he felt before he began his forty-day challenge. "I felt constant shame and guilt. I was feeding my addiction and trying to get rid of it at the same time. I even thought that getting married might be the answer to my problem. I quickly found out that no matter what I did, my addiction always seemed to have the upper hand. I knew that if I was ever going to truly be free, I would need a different approach."

As Tom began his forty days, he started by removing the things that were feeding his addiction. Pornographic magazines, websites, and places he used to frequent were no longer options. He started putting up guardrails to keep himself away from anything that would act as fuel. "I had to get myself out of and away from that destructive lifestyle," he said.

When I spoke with him, Tom had gone without pornography for forty-two days. Tom told me that now, for the first time in his life, he has self-esteem. "I can look at myself in mirror with confidence instead of shame," he said. Tom's marriage too is better and his spiritual connection is much stronger. Perhaps best of all, Tom said, "I no longer have a constant cloud of guilt hanging over my head."

PART II

PROGRESS IS MORE IMPORTANT THAN PERFECTION

For a just man falls seven times and rises up again.
—**PROVERBS 24:16**

The anger of the LORD was inflamed against Israel, and He made them wander in the wilderness forty years, until all the generation that did evil in the eyes of the LORD was finished.
—**NUMBERS 32:13**

If you look for perfection, you'll never be satisfied.[1]
—**LEO TOLSTOY**

Day 5

PROGRESS, NOT PERFECTION

Occasionally, as we set out toward change, we fall back into old patterns. This is often called relapse. Relapse is not fatal unless it takes us out of the fight. Not winning every battle is better than losing the war. Today concentrate on those areas where you are still faltering. Decide to come up higher.

Key Verse: *For a just man falls seven times and rises up again.*
—PROVERBS 24:16

A S YOU CONTINUE on this forty-day journey, keep in mind that progress, not perfection, is the goal. It took thousands of years for a single river to carve out the Grand Canyon, and it would be impossible to take it back to its original state in one day. You are on a quest to transform your future behavior by focusing on changing your old patterns of behavior. As you move through the remainder of your forty days, don't get discouraged and quit just because conditions are not perfect.

I have a feeling the last four days have felt like a roller-coaster ride. One second you are up and the next the bottom falls out. Perfection has been elusive. Maybe before breakfast on day one you were on track on your forty-day quest of self-confrontation, but by lunch you had already messed up. What you renounced, you once again embraced.

Relax, it's all right. Just take a deep breath, regroup, and start again. I remember teaching my oldest son, Trent, to ride a bicycle. He had a terrible time getting it right. He would fall over just about every time he tried, but we never gave up. I ran down the street beside him for blocks holding on to the seat, and each time I let go, over he went. There were lots of scraped knees and elbows, but he just kept getting back on that bike. One day as we were having our usual run, I let go...and he kept riding without me.

That was a great day because what he could not do on his own the previous day he was now doing all by himself. In your journey God is running beside you. He is the dad with His hand on the bicycle seat who is not going to turn loose until you can ride on your own. After my son learned to ride, there were still occasions when he fell over. As his father, I didn't disown him or tell him he was a failure. No, I helped him up, brushed him off, and sent him back on his way.

Just because you can't do it today, doesn't mean you won't be able to do it tomorrow. Any time you're trying to do the right thing, God will help you, partner with you, and come alongside you, and together you will be able to do it.

This is a lesson that the nation of Israel failed to realize. Their reluctance to regroup and start again with God's help would backfire. We read in Numbers 32:13:

> The anger of the LORD was inflamed against Israel, and He made them wander in the wilderness forty years, until all the generation that did evil in the eyes of the LORD was finished.

Though God had miraculously brought them out of Egypt, the children of Israel never learned, never grew past where they were, and never trusted or completely followed God. They blamed Moses, and they blamed their circumstances. In the face of opposition they constantly wanted to return to their old way of life, and they often ignored the progress they were making. As a result, they never made it out of the desert.

God was trying to take them to destiny and blessing, but all they could remember was their former life in Egypt. Slavery was the only life they had ever known. Canaan was the destination, but Egypt was always on their minds.

I have always thought it interesting that Canaan was described as the land flowing with milk and honey (Num. 13:27), and Egypt was described as the land of onions and garlic (Num. 11:5). Wow, the only thing between you and the life you want might be garlic breath! No thanks. Give me milk and honey over garlic.

Egypt was the place of slavery and cruel taskmasters deciding your every move. Canaan was the place of freedom and abundance. Egypt stinks, but Canaan has a sweet aroma. Don't get hung up on the garlic of your past. God has a sweet future for you!

During their forty-year march the Israelites did all the wrong things, and as a result they died in the wilderness—but their story did not have to end that way. Their stinky past could have been replaced with a sweet future if only they had focused on how far they had come rather than on how far they still had to go. Progress was ignored.

Then the LORD said to Moses, "Go down, because your people, whom you brought up out of Egypt, have become corrupt. They have been quick to turn away from what I commanded them and have made themselves an idol cast in the shape of a calf. They have bowed down to it and sacrificed to it and have said, 'These are your gods, Israel, who brought you up out of Egypt.'"

—EXODUS 32:7–8, NIV

Moses had been gone for forty days (Exod. 24:18) and in that brief time Israel was "quick to turn away" (Exod. 32:8). In less than forty days they had already forgotten about their commitment to reach for a better life. The result was catastrophic. They lacked focus!

As we have discussed, Jesus also spent time in the wilderness (Luke 4). God watched as He locked horns with His flesh and proved Himself worthy to take our place on the cross. It was an unimaginable struggle, but unlike Israel, Jesus resisted, outwitted, and used the Word to fight against temptation. Jesus confronted Himself and the desires of His flesh. As a result, the Bible says Satan left (Luke 4:13).

Wouldn't it be great to wake up in the morning to find the opponent you've been fighting for years suddenly gone? Those feelings of rejection gone, those extra pounds gone, those poisonous thoughts gone, fear gone, loneliness gone, habits gone, and insecurity gone—all of it gone! That does not happen by accident. Jesus, unlike Israel, continued to make progress even though the Devil was relentless in his assault. You can be the person who dies in the wilderness or you can be the person whose opposition leaves.

If you are going to make the progress necessary to have the future you want, you're going to have to continue to march forward even when your circumstances are less than perfect. Let's move onward and upward.

REFLECTION JOURNAL

Have you given up on changing yourself all because of your inability to get it perfect? Will you continue to move forward despite the fact that you are still falling down?

_____

_____

_____

_____

_____

_____

_____

_____

_____

_____

_____

_____

_____

_____

Day 6

WHAT IS POSSESSING YOUR PROMISED LAND?

The Devil is a trespasser. He quickly learned in Eden that all he needs to affect our lives is to spend some time in our backyards. Expect to challenge the limits your devils have illegally imposed upon your life. Get the snake out of your garden!

Key Verse: *Then Caleb silenced the people before Moses and said, "We should go up and take possession of the land, for we can certainly do it."*
—NUMBERS 13:30, NIV

IN NUMBERS CHAPTER 13 we find the children of Israel nearing the end of their forty-year journey through the wilderness. God in His mercy is giving them one last chance to make the changes necessary to enter the destiny He had prepared for them. They are literally standing on the border of the Promised Land. I have a feeling that if the wind was blowing in the right direction they probably could have smelled the Rose of Sharon that was growing just on the other side.

This story might be typical of your life. Maybe you have been so close so many times but have never truly been able to enter into the future you want. Maybe you have read books like this one or possibly heard sermons about the Israelites missing out when they were so close to their promised land, but for you that future has never been a reality. In your dreams you are sitting by a brook dipping your toes in the cool water and eating honeycomb, but in reality you're walking in a desert chewing the garlic of your past.

Before doing what God told them to do, which was to be intentional and take possession of their promise, the Israelites decided to send in some spies to see if the land could be taken from the enemies who were already living there. Sadly this is all too true in the lives of many of God's people. We never make it to our Canaan because we feel as if our devils are already living there. Be prepared but don't give your enemies a heads-up. *Don't survey your enemies before you decide to attack them!*

> At the end of forty days they returned from exploring the land. They came back to Moses and Aaron and the whole Israelite community at Kadesh in the Desert of Paran. There they reported to them and to the whole assembly and showed them the fruit of the land. They gave Moses this account: "We went into the land to which you sent us, and it does flow with milk and honey! Here is its fruit. But the people who live there are powerful, and the cities are fortified and very large. We even saw the descendants of Anak there. The Amalekites live in the Negev; the Hittites, Jebusites and the Amorites live in the hill country; and the Canaanites live near the sea and along the Jordan."
>
> —NUMBERS 13:25–29, NIV

All but two of the spies returning from Canaan said, "We can't do it; the opposition is too strong." They saw everything from Christmas lights to mosquito bites in the land! There was no shortage of -ites! The enemy was large and fortified, and the spies believed they could not win. The end result was catastrophic. The majority of the people died in the wilderness.

For forty days they needed the right attitude. For forty days they needed a resolve that said, "We can do this." For forty days they should have been making plans for victory. However, that was not the case in this story. They spent their forty days surveying the opposition instead of preparing to move. Your devil will never admit to you that you could actually defeat it.

Instead of focusing on the sheer size of the enemy, what if they had focused on the land flowing with milk and honey? Yes, the enemy was large and the fight would be fierce, but the reward would have been worth it.

I would like to think that if it had been me, I would have spent those forty days picking out a spot to build my new house. I would have been checking out the local rivers to see which ones would be best for fishing! I would have hooked up a U-Haul to my camel! I would have been making plans to move! I hope, as Caleb and Joshua did, I would have said, "Come on guys, we can do this!"

The spies said what we say so often: "It's too hard and the opposition is too great. We have studied the enemy, and our observation tells us this is a battle we cannot win."

Our enemies range from failed dieting to abuse and trauma from our childhood, and in many cases we decide that we can never have a future because it has already been occupied by our opposition. Just as Israel recognized the Hittites, we recognize our insecurity. Just as Israel recognized the Jebusites, we recognize our familiar habits and addictions.

The spies even mentioned the descendants of Anak. These were giant-size opponents, and except for Caleb and Joshua, the spies could only see how big their opposition was. They had already forgotten how big God was! By this time they had already seen miracle after miracle, but as is sometimes the case with us, the problems seemed to overshadow the solutions. This same group had seen God part the Red Sea, send quail knee-deep into the camp, and bring water out of a rock. Despite the past provision, the enemy seemed too daunting. That's because they paid more attention to the enemy than to God.

Don't be like the Israelites. *Don't spy on the enemy. Prepare for battle.*

REFLECTION JOURNAL

Consider your opposition. Do your devils currently occupy positions key to your recovery? How will you approach and invade those areas where the enemy is trespassing?

Day 7

REVERSE YOUR BEHAVIOR
AND CHANGE YOUR LIFE

Expect to do some reminiscing today. Decide
to learn from the mistakes of your past rather
than continuing to circle back to them.

Key Verse: *Only do not rebel against the Lord, nor
fear the people of the land.... Their defense is gone from
them, and the Lord is with us. Do not fear them.*
—Numbers 13:9

WE READ IN Numbers 14:34: "For forty years—one
year for each of the forty days you explored the
land—you will suffer for your sins and know what it is like
to have me against you" (NIV). This is a sobering verse. God
was telling the nation of Israel, "Because you chose to do
the wrong thing for forty days, it's going to affect your next
forty years."

While God is full of mercy and forgiveness, He does
not always deliver us from the consequences we sometimes
create. The expedition of spies to the Promised Land would
only reinforce this important truth.

How do you want to spend the next forty years? How
about taking a stand against the familiar enemies that are
usurping your future? How would that affect your life?

Maybe you are like my friend John who spent the first
twenty years of his adult life in prison due to a powerful

drug addiction. He, like the nation of Israel, learned the hard way that when you spend days participating in wrong behavior, it can lead you into years of pain and devastation. John is now the associate pastor at a large metropolitan church in the South. He is proof that when you reverse your behavior, you can change your future. What you do during your forty-day challenge—the patterns you establish—can be used as a guide to help you for the rest of your life. That is why it is so important that you continue on.

Now that you have reached day 7 of this challenge, it is imperative that you have a mental picture of what you desire for your future. This is called a vision.

By now you no doubt have a glimpse of what life could be like if the devil wreaking havoc in your life was served an eviction notice. Take a few minutes and write out your vision. What do you want your life to look like? Write as if it has already happened. Don't think about what was, think about what could be. As Scripture says, "Write the vision, and make it plain" (Hab. 2:2).

My life vision is:

_____

_____

_____

I encourage you to read this vision every day for the remainder of your forty days. By doing this, you will begin to see yourself in a whole new light. The person you want to be will begin to take shape in your mind.

One thing you will need in order to accomplish this is to change your "I can't" mentality into an attitude like Caleb's. When everyone else was saying, "We can't defeat our enemies in the Promised Land. It's too hard. This is impossible," Caleb was saying something different. The fortified cities and the giant-size opponents were of little to no consequence to him.

Caleb was looking for more than he had. He was a man on a mission, and nothing would stop him. He knew the question wasn't, "Can we do it?" The question was, "Will we do it?"

> Then Caleb silenced the people before Moses and said, "We should go up and take possession of the land, for we can certainly do it."
>
> —Numbers 13:30, niv

When everyone around him was concentrating on why they couldn't, his attitude was, "Why can't we?" When everyone else was thinking about how hard it would be to move into a better future, he was thinking about the reward of doing what it would take to get there. When everyone else was focusing on everything but God, Caleb was focusing on God and nothing else! Preparing your mind for battle is the first step to victory.

There were no doubt times in Caleb's past when battles had been lost, but not this time and not today. Caleb had a laser focus, and he refused to be distracted. The enemy was big, but God was bigger. The outcome would not be based upon the size of Caleb's enemy but rather on the size of Caleb's God. And make no mistake, God took notice.

> Say to them, "As I live," says the LORD, "just as you have spoken in My ears, so I will do to you. In this wilderness your corpses will fall, and all who were numbered of you, according to your whole number, from twenty years old and upward, who have murmured against Me, you will not go into the land which I swore by My hand to cause you to dwell in it, except Caleb the son of Jephunneh and Joshua the son of Nun."
> —NUMBERS 14:28–30

If you don't think forty days of doing what's right matters, just ask Caleb and Joshua. They were the only two who had the right focus the previous forty days, and they were the only members of their generation who entered the Promised Land. Everyone else who possessed the land was twenty years old or younger.

Have you picked out a spot in the promised land to build your new home? Are you ready for a change of scenery? It's time to turn your can'ts into cans and your dreams into plans! It's time for you to look past the enemies of yesterday and see the life God has arranged for you.

Progress happens in your life when, like Caleb, you decide that you certainly can! The completion of any journey starts with a decision to take the first step. As it is with a toddler, our steps do not have to be pretty to be progress. Even baby steps will take you somewhere!

REFLECTION JOURNAL

Think about the areas where you have reaped the negative consequences of your behavior. How will you guard yourself so you don't circle back?

_____

_____

_____

_____

_____

_____

_____

_____

_____

_____

_____

_____

_____

_____

_____

_____

_____

_____

Day 8

GIVE UP YOUR WAYS

Progress can be difficult when you are stubborn.
Today reflect on Jonah's three-day cruise
inside the fish. If God sends you a fish, make
sure it's on a bun with tartar sauce!

Key Verse: *Let everyone call urgently on God. Let them give up their evil ways and their violence.*
—JONAH 3:8, NIV

CALL ON GOD and give up your ways. It's time to change!" That was Jonah's message to the people of Nineveh, and that's God's message to you.

After Jonah's famous three-day cruise in the belly of the great fish, he ended up in Nineveh, a godless city known for its wickedness. The Bible tells us:

> Jonah began to enter the city, going a day's walk. And he cried out, "In forty days' time, Nineveh will be overthrown!"... Then he made a proclamation in Nineveh: "...Both man and animals shall cover themselves with sackcloth and cry mightily to God. All shall turn from their evil ways and from the violence that is in their hands." [Notice that here again we see the number forty, which is deeply connected to the process of turning from our former behavior and turning to God.]
> —JONAH 3:4, 7–8

Ironically, before Jonah gave this shocking pronouncement in Nineveh, he had the same problem as the people in this great city. He did not want to do what was necessary to secure his future. So before Jonah could convince the Ninevites to give up their ungodly ways, God had to convince Jonah to give up his.

Before you pray, "Your kingdom come," you'd better be prepared to pray, "My kingdom go." Before Jonah was ready to walk in his future, some changes had to take place. Only when Jonah got the point that he was ready to give up his ways was he prepared to convince others to give up their ways as well.

From inside the fish, Jonah finally realized he had been settling for a life of second best. Looking at the rib cage of that fish caused him to wake up to the fact that he had been living in a self-imposed prison, and he said, "My life is ebbing away." (See Jonah 2:7.)

Is that how you feel? Is your life passing by without you in it? Maybe you are like my friend Keith. By giving in to his personal devils, he wasted many years of his life. He told me, "Larry, I might as well have just lit my life on fire, because in the last five years everything that I touched burned to the ground."

I am happy to report that Keith is back on track and as a result, God is restoring all that was lost. Keith made it out of the fish's belly and so can you!

After running from God's call and spending three days in the belly of the fish, Jonah looked up to heaven and said, "What I have vowed I will make good" (Jon. 2:9, NIV).

Jonah told God he would make the sacrifice. Riding around in a fish's belly makes for a stinky life. Jonah wanted something more, and he was prepared to pay the price for it.

The people of Nineveh believed Jonah when he told them that if they didn't give up their ways, disaster would strike in forty days. (Who knows, he might have even been passing out copies of this book!) Suddenly an urgency took them over, and from the greatest to the smallest they decided to give God at least the next forty days of their lives to see if calamity could be avoided.

> So the people of Nineveh believed God, and proclaimed a fast. And everyone, great and small, put on sackcloth.... When God saw their actions, that they turned from their evil ways, He changed His mind about the disaster that He had said He would bring upon them, and He did not do it.
>
> —JONAH 3:5, 10

They became urgent about changing their behavior. The word *urgent* means very important and needing immediate action. It was time for them to get serious about changing, and for them, changing meant turning from some of the things they had become accustomed to.

I would say your life is probably not a picture of the evil that was occurring in Nineveh, but I would also say you probably have areas where you need to do some turning. The people of Nineveh changed their ways and turned their behavior around for forty days, and destruction was averted. But it happened only because the people believed, got a sense of urgency, and changed.

That is the secret to unlocking the life you have been looking for. Believe, get a sense of urgency, and change! *No one is born a winner, and no one is born a loser. We are all born choosers.*

REFLECTION JOURNAL

Describe those areas where you have a sense of urgency when it comes to change. What would the consequences be if you decided not to give up your ways?

_____

_____

_____

_____

_____

_____

_____

_____

_____

_____

_____

_____

_____

Real People, Real Stories

Carl's Story

Carl, a new Christian, would use his forty-day challenge to develop spiritual habits. "I wanted to grow and be more like Christ," he said, "but praying and reading the Bible were never a part of my lifestyle. I needed something to help get me jump-started."

Carl began by taking an honest look at his life. His spiritual condition was not where he wanted it to be. This is what Carl had to say about the days leading up to his forty-day challenge: "I felt lost and confused when it came to reading Scripture. I was also not making time every day to pray and connect with God. The old, familiar routines were hard to break."

On the first day of the challenge Carl went to a Christian bookstore and picked up a devotional written by Billy Graham. Glancing through the pages, he began to see a plan that might work. Every day for forty days he would read the devotional and spend time in prayer.

Progress was slow at first, and there were days in the beginning when he either ran out of time or simply forgot to spend quality time with God. He soon, however, developed a routine, and before long Carl had created a lifestyle that allowed him to connect with God every day.

Months later Carl is still studying Scripture and is now praying twice daily. He feels stronger in his faith, and for the first time sees himself as a role model to his young daughter. He credits the daily Scripture reading and prayer time as the push he needed to not return to his old way of life.

"This challenge helped me develop spiritual disciplines," he said. "Sometimes new believers need an extra nudge to get them moving in the right direction."

PART III

DON'T TRY TO SAVE WHAT GOD'S TRYING TO DROWN

In seven days I will cause it to rain on the earth for forty days and forty nights, and every living thing that I have made I will destroy from the face of the earth.

—GENESIS 7:4

Since, then, we do not have the excuse of ignorance, everything—and I do mean everything—connected with that old way of life has to go. It's rotten through and through. Get rid of it! And then take on an entirely new way of life—a God-fashioned life, a life renewed from the inside and working itself into your conduct as God accurately reproduces his character in you.

—EPHESIANS 4:22–24, THE MESSAGE

Day 9

THERE WERE NO LIFEGUARDS ON THE ARK

Sometimes negative behavior feels as comfortable as your favorite pair of old jeans. You can slip them on without much effort. Today decide to drown those "go-to" behaviors that keep your life feeling stale.

Key Verse: *Since, then, we do not have the excuse of ignorance, everything, and I do mean everything connected with that old way of life has to go. It's rotten through and through. Get rid of it!*
—EPHESIANS 4:22, THE MESSAGE

S PRING IS WITHOUT a doubt my favorite time of the year. After months of frozen landscapes I am always ready for the Ozark hills to wake up. Bare trees and the brown grass aren't nearly as exciting as fresh blooms and busy hummingbirds. What winter cleanses, spring brings back. The old vanishes as the new takes its place. This was precisely what God was teaching Noah.

Sometimes we feel as if our lives are in a perpetual state of winter. There is nothing new, nothing green. It is just the same old barrenness. Maybe the reason the new hasn't arrived is because you haven't yet gotten rid of the old. Just like the sleeping trees, it is time for you to wake up.

The familiar patterns of our past can become comfortable. The old is cozy. We get used to it, and before long we settle into a life we don't really want. Days become weeks, weeks become months, and months become years. We look back and wonder where our lives went.

There is a certain amount of letting go required of all of us if we are going to move into the future we truly want. Noah certainly learned this.

> In seven days I will cause it to rain on the earth for forty days and forty nights, and every living thing that I have made I will destroy from the face of the earth.
>
> —GENESIS 7:4

The number forty is connected to cleansing and getting rid of the old in order to establish the new. If you are going to move to another level of living, God will require you to let go of some things. Just as the trees must drop their leaves in the fall before they can bloom in the spring, you will be required to let some things fall from your life. The forest floor is always cluttered with what used to be so that there can be room for what has never been.

God will require you to let go. It might be as simple as letting go of a McDonald's french fry, or it might be as difficult as letting go of the hurt someone else intentionally inflicted upon you. Whatever the case, God will require you to intentionally turn some things loose.

Are you willing to let go of what God is trying to eliminate from your life? This can be very difficult, because it has been a part of you for so long. In order to stop repeating the same cycle of failure, are you willing to allow the dead, brown leaves of the past to fall so your life can bloom?

> In the six hundredth year of Noah's life, in the second
> month, on the seventeenth day of the month, the same
> day, all the fountains of the great deep burst open and
> the floodgates of the heavens were opened. The rain fell
> upon the earth for forty days and forty nights.
> —GENESIS 7:11–12

This is a very familiar Bible story. It is an amazing tale
of obedience and radical faith. Yes, there are rainbows, animals arriving in pairs, and a big boat that became a floating
zoo, but the message is that of unwavering obedience.

God said to Noah, "It is going to rain on the earth for
forty days and forty nights, and everything except for the
people and animals in the ark are going to be obliterated."
The rain would be destructive, and everything except what
God set apart would die. This may seem like an extreme
response to the problem, but it was crucial that the old go
so the new could come. The two could not coexist.

The earth was a beautiful paradise at this time. Yes, the
fall of Adam and Eve brought thorns to the garden, but the
earth was still in pristine condition. Of course, God didn't
want to destroy the earth, but man had become so wicked
that He became sorry He had ever created humanity. God
had to do what so many of us need to do. He had to start
over, but before He could start over there first had to be a
cleansing and a lot of things had to go.

There were no lifeguards on the ark.

About two thousand years passed between creation
and the flood, and I am sure God had a lot invested in
the earth by this time. But it was still time to start over.

The fact that you've invested time in something doesn't always mean it's worth keeping.

God knew if things were going to get better, He would have to take immediate action. He couldn't sit around with His fingers crossed hoping for change. Man had demonstrated that he was not going to improve on his own. As difficult as it would be, it was time for some things to drown.

Are you willing to let some things drown in your life? Before the new can come, the old has to go.

REFLECTION JOURNAL

Consider the time you have spent entertaining your devil. Do you see it as time invested or as time wasted? How would your calendar look if you allowed your devil to drown?

_____

_____

_____

_____

_____

_____

_____

_____

_____

_____

Day 10

YOUR OLD LIFE AND NEW LIFE CANNOT COEXIST

The great flood in Noah's day was not a scene
from the movie *Titanic*. There were no lifeboats.
Everything in the water had to drown. Today
expect to hear devils calling from outside the
ark, wanting to be rescued. Refuse them.

Key Verse: *No one pours new wine into old wineskins.*
—MARK 2:22

OUR GOD IS long-suffering, but eventually even His
patience wears out. This was the case for Noah's generation. The Bible tells us:

The LORD saw that the wickedness of man was great
on the earth, and that every intent of the thoughts of
his heart was continually only evil. The LORD was sorry
that He had made man on the earth, and it grieved Him
in His heart. So the LORD said, "I will destroy man,
whom I have created, from the face of the earth—both
man and beast, and the creeping things, and the birds of
the sky, for I am sorry that I have made them."
—GENESIS 6:5–7

After God gives us chance after chance, He will do
whatever it takes to save us from ourselves. That includes
letting some things drown. Make no mistake: *you will never*

become successful by investing time in things God is trying to drown.

What destructive behavior do you keep performing CPR on? I would guess it's probably one of those issues that motivated you to pick up this book. Although we understand we must let go of negative behaviors connected to our past, many times we are on the deck of the ark throwing lifelines to the things God is trying to drown.

Imagine if Noah or his sons were out on the deck of the ark trying to rescue the people struggling in the water. The flood wasn't a scene from the movie *Titanic*. There were no lifeboats and no rescue ships. Everyone and everything in the water had to go. It was more like a scene from *The Perfect Storm*. The wind, waves, and water would simply be too much for anyone not on the ark. Once God shut the door, no one could get in and no one could get out. Before the new could come, the old had to be washed away.

Too often this is a picture of our own lives. We are desperately trying to save the things that God says have to go in order for us to move on, have better relationships, and be at peace with who we are. We want the new, because we know it will lead us to the life we desperately want, but we are grasping the old with white-knuckle determination. The fact is, *your old life and your new life simply cannot coexist.*

Jesus said it like this, "No one pours new wine into old wineskins. Otherwise, the wine will burst the skins, and both the wine and the wineskins will be ruined. No, they pour new wine into new wineskins" (Mark 2:22, NIV). In other words, you can't put the new life God has for you into the old wineskins of your old way of living. Your old life and your new life simply cannot live together.

What do you keep trying to save? Is it an addiction, a poisonous relationship, a habit, an unhealthy lifestyle, or maybe a grudge you have been holding for years?

As you spend these forty days cleansing your life, *be ready for the wind, rain, and waves that come with the cleansing.* Your flesh will beg, "Save me! Save me!" You are going to hear nicotine calling out, "Help, I'm drowning!" You are going to hear cravings for food calling out, "I'm going under!" You are going to hear the voice of resentment and bitterness calling, "You can't let us go."

When that happens, you have a choice to make: Do you suffer through the violence of the cleanse or do you settle for the life you have always had? Choose to suffer!

> Then at the end of forty days, Noah opened the window
> of the ark which he had made.
> —GENESIS 8:6

When the storm was finally over and the violence of the cleanse was behind them, the ark came to rest on the top of a mountain, but Noah waited another forty days before opening the window. Can you imagine traveling with your family and your pets in the car for about a year, and when you finally reach your destination you announce that everyone will be sitting in the car for another forty days? In my family I am afraid there would be a mutiny!

So why on earth would Noah wait another forty days to leave the ark? It was because the water had to recede.

The familiar sky, I am sure, brought Noah and his family comfort, but even more comforting was the fact that they were being given a fresh start.

Why did it rain for forty days and forty nights? We don't know. What we do know is that when the rain quit falling and the ark quit floating, Noah waited forty more days before he exited. It's as if he was wanted to give God forty more days to ensure he got the transition right.

Will you stop trying to save the people, habits, and behaviors that God is trying to cleanse from your life? When the rain starts falling and your flesh begins to drown, will you push past your usual behavior and make the progress you have been dreaming about?

REFLECTION JOURNAL

After you nail your devil to the cross and say, "Never again," do you resurrect it every few days? How will you change that?

_____

_____

_____

_____

_____

_____

_____

_____

_____

Day 11

WHAT IF NOAH HAD SAID NO?

You've spent more than ten days in this challenge, and
your devils are beginning to panic. The fact that you
are still saying yes to a better future concerns them.
Boat building is tiring, but keep in mind that you are
building more than an ark. You are building your future!

Key Verse: *I can do all things because
of Christ who strengthens me.*
—PHILIPPIANS 4:13

CAN YOU IMAGINE what it must have been like to be
Noah? He lived in the most godless society on record,
and yet somehow he managed to walk with God for six
hundred years. Sometimes I struggle to walk with God a
week at a time!

I have often pictured Noah out in the front yard, building
a ship the size of two football fields. He must have been the
talk of the town, especially since he lived miles from the
nearest large body of water. That's not to mention the fact
that at this time in history, the people of the earth had never
even seen rain, let alone a flood! I am sure the neighbor-
hood kids regularly stopped by to harass crazy old Noah, the
doomsday preacher and professional boat builder.

But Noah had heard God clearly say:

I will bring a flood of waters on the earth to destroy all
flesh, wherever there is the breath of life under heaven,

and everything that is on the earth will die. But I will establish My covenant with you; you must go into the ark—you, and your sons, and your wife, and your sons' wives with you.

—Genesis 6:17–18

But what if Noah had said, "The task is too daunting; I can't do it"? He could easily have done that. After all, the task did seem impossible. Building the ark would require sacrifice, discipline, and a complete shift in Noah's lifestyle. Noah still said yes.

God is probably not going to ask you to build another ark, but the adjustments you are trying to make might seem just as impossible. Remember this: *you will never succeed until you say yes to whatever it is you believe you cannot do.*

You have a choice: you can drown your flesh, bad habits, and old ways of self-sabotage, or you can drown your future by saying no. It's up to you.

I'd suggest *you make yourself an ark.*

So make yourself an ark of cypress wood; make rooms in it and coat it with pitch inside and out.

—Genesis 6:14, niv

No one was going to be able to do this for Noah. There was no Ark Building 101 down at the local community college. There is no record of Noah even being a carpenter.

If the boat carrying you to the future shows up, it will be because you decided to build it. God is always willing to provide on-the-job training when it comes to ark building, but you must pick up the hammer. *It's time to make yourself an ark.*

Ark building is tough work, just as it will be tough for you to make the changes you need to make. It took Noah one hundred years to build his ark. You're only sacrificing forty days. As tough as it may be at times, remember, through this forty-day journey you are actually building your future. With every tree chopped down, with every bucket of tar gathered, Noah was building more than a boat. Noah was building a new life. So are you.

Take the initiative. Make steps to change. *Don't wait for God to put an end to it.*

> So God said to Noah, "I am going to put an end to all people."
>
> —GENESIS 6:13, NIV

At some point God said, "Enough is enough. I am going to end this. Man is not going to get better on his own." The Lord had patiently watched and waited, but instead of changing, man gradually sank into more and more depravity.

What if the people in the story of Noah and the ark had put an end to their behavior before God had to involve Himself? What if others had joined Noah in his ark building adventure? What if change would have come before the inevitable consequences? Sadly we will never know because this story has already been written.

Your story, however, is not yet finished. It is still being penned! In your story change can come before consequences! You can put an end to your usual behavior, and that begins with your thoughts.

Did you know that your heart can think? The Bible says,

"The LORD saw that the wickedness of man was great on the earth, and that every intent of the *thoughts of his heart* was continually only evil" (Gen. 6:5, emphasis added).

Before the forty-day cleansing of the earth, God turned His attention to the thoughts occurring in the hearts of mankind. Noah was the only one with a heart that was thinking right thoughts, and as a result he and his family were the only ones who would have a future.

Your future greatly depends upon how you view the issues of your past. If you believe a task is too daunting—it is. If you believe you are up to the challenge—you are.

Either way, you will get what you believe. The people who were swept away in the flood were not unlike us. Their outward behavior was really just a reflection of their internal thoughts. This is not a book on the power of the mind. But if your life is going to change during this forty-day journey, your thinking will need to change as well.

> Above all else, guard your heart, for everything you do flows from it.
> —PROVERBS 4:23, NIV

Your heart must be guarded. You can choose to think about all the times you started building an ark only to quit halfway though, or the times you actually thought you had it built only to drive it into a mountain and watch it sink. Or you can choose not to focus on those failed ark-building adventures and put all your efforts into forty days that could change everything!

REFLECTION JOURNAL

Why do you believe there are some things that are just impossible for you to accomplish? Have you considered saying yes to the impossible?

_____

_____

_____

_____

_____

_____

_____

_____

_____

_____

_____

_____

_____

_____

_____

_____

_____

Day 12

THE REWARD OF SAYING YES

Saying yes can be frightening, especially when you are moving out into uncharted waters. Don't allow the unknown to keep you from setting sail. Anchors aweigh!

Key Verse: *Noah did this; he did all that God commanded him.*

—GENESIS 6:22

WITHOUT A DOUBT, I can tell you that my greatest accomplishments and most rewarding achievements were a result of saying yes to something that I honestly would have liked to have said no to. Over the years God has asked me to say yes on more than one occasion. In everything from overseeing the construction of multimillion-dollar building programs to moving hundreds of miles to help struggling congregations, yes is the answer God was looking for.

In each case I had no way of knowing what the outcome would be. I had to trust that where I was going would be better than where I had been. God doesn't always give us details concerning the future. We have to trust Him, and that can be difficult, especially when we are dabbling in the unknown. Experience has taught me that if God asks me to go somewhere or to complete an assignment, He pays more than minimum wage!

When Noah agreed to build the ark, the directive was clear: gather your family along with the animals and stay alive.

71

> But I will establish My covenant with you; you must go
> into the ark—you, and your sons, and your wife, and your
> sons' wives with you. Bring every living thing of all flesh,
> two of every kind, into the ark to keep them alive with you.
> —GENESIS 6:18–19

There is no mention of a reward. Survival was the only
reward on the table at this moment. Noah would have to
trust God to sweeten the deal once the work was done. It
must have been difficult to say yes with only the promise
of covenant, but Noah said yes anyway. There was no guar-
antee of what life would look like the on the other side of
the flood. Would it be better? Would it be worse? There
was no way to tell. It was uncharted territory. In Noah's
mind it must have seemed like a gamble.

Noah had not yet seen the rainbow.

Remember, at this point God had not shared His dream
for the future with Noah. God could have said, "Look up,
Noah. Do you see that colorful arch in the sky? It's called
a rainbow. That is what will be waiting for you after this
flood is over." God did not offer proof of a reward. On the
contrary, He had only explained the nightmare that was
to come. God spoke of death and drowning, not future
blessing and abundance.

Noah was saying yes to an unknown future. He would
maintain his relationship with his immediate family, but
everything else familiar to him would be washed away.
There was nothing easy about signing on to the plan.

After all was said and done and the new first family

exited the ark, the reward of saying yes would be all around them. Now it would be easy to say, "That was worth it."

When they exited the ark, God told them:

> "And as for you, be fruitful and multiply; increase abundantly in the earth and multiply in it." Again God spoke to Noah and to his sons with him, saying, "As for Me, I establish My covenant with you, and with your descendants after you....I have set My rainbow in the cloud, and it shall be a sign of a covenant between Me and the earth."
>
> —Genesis 9:7–9, 13

One yes to God can erase a thousand nos. The reward of saying yes will extend far beyond your current circumstances. Noah's entire family benefited from his willingness to say, "I don't know where You're taking me, Father, but I am in!" Noah realized that where he was going would be better than where he was. He didn't have to know the future to start working toward it.

You may have no idea what your life will look like if you say yes to God. Maybe you are still holding on to the familiar devils of your past because outside of them all you can see is a meager existence. Like the drug addict who is only focused on the symptoms of withdrawal rather than the reward of getting clean, you see only consequences.

Noah would not be forced to live on a stinky ark for the rest of his life. No, the ark was the vehicle God used to carry him to the destination He had in mind. Noah said yes to temporary discomfort because he had a hope for better days. Saying yes doesn't mean there won't be consequences and temporary pain, because there will be. Saying yes, however, will cause you to eventually get to the end of the rainbow. Whatever God ask of you today, say yes!

The waters may be uncharted to you, but remember, they are not uncharted to God. He knew what He had in mind for both Noah and the earth before one drop of rain ever fell from the sky. You can trust Him with your future.

REFLECTION JOURNAL

What do you fear most about the future? Have you considered that the future God has in mind for you might just be what you have been looking for all along?

Real People, Real Stories

Scott and Susan's Story

Susan and her husband, Scott, did not begin following Christ until they were in their late thirties. They have spent the last ten years learning to both trust and surrender their lives to Him. But taking this forty-day challenge would test the limits of their obedience. It is worth noting that I interviewed them on day forty-one.

Susan and Scott used their forty-day challenge to focus on making their lives less complicated so they could spend more time with each other and have more time to serve in their church. They had no idea the amount of sacrifice this would require. "Our schedules were overwhelming and we felt constant stress," Susan said. "If this were to change, my husband, Scott, would be required to quit his job."

Scott was the regional manager for a large company and earned a six-figure salary. On top of working ten-hour days, Scott also had a two-hour commute. Working from home on both nights and weekends was common. "We had no time to invest in our marriage or in our ministry," Scott said.

As difficult as it was, Scott quit his job. He decided that chasing life was more important than chasing money. Taking the forty-day journey was the perfect opportunity for him to step out in faith and trust God to provide the future that he and his wife both wanted. "We knew that it would not be easy and would require tremendous sacrifice," Susan explained, "but we also knew that Scott's career path had become our devil."

After Scott quit his job, they relied heavily upon the teaching in this book. "It helped us maintain our belief that God was with us as we faced this uphill battle," Scott said. "It kept us focused on the result we wanted rather than the excuses we had always relied upon in the past."

"We learned that you can talk yourself out of anything that your flesh doesn't want to do," Susan added. "So we asked God to help us kill our flesh and do this."

Their forty-day challenge taught them that it is one thing to say you believe in God and another thing to completely trust Him with your life. By the time they reached the end of the journey, Scott already had multiple job offers. He decided to take a job that allows him to work from home. He and Susan can now spend quality time together, and Scott can devote more of his time to ministry.

This is what Scott and Susan had to say concerning the concepts they learned through the forty-day challenge. "Obedience is the first step to the future. Everything you have been chasing comes after that. This challenge pushed us to do what we should have done years ago. We are excited about the new chapter of our lives and realize that none of it would have been possible if we were not willing to let go of the old."

PART IV

IT'S JUST THE USUAL

As he was talking with them, Goliath, the Philistine champion from Gath, stepped out from his lines and shouted his usual *defiance, and David heard it.*

—1 SAMUEL 17:23, NIV, EMPHASIS ADDED

At my age, I do what Mark Twain did. I get my daily paper, look at the obituaries page, and if I am not there I carry on as usual.[1]

—SIR PATRICK MOORE

Day 13

THE USUAL DEFIANCE

You will never become the person you want to be
by providing the bullets for the gun your flesh will
use to shoot you. Why not do something unusual
today, such as deciding to abandon the "usual."

Key Verse: *Make no provision for the flesh to fulfill its lusts.*
—ROMANS 13:14

MANY TIMES IN life we find ourselves facing the same
opposition over and over. The calendar may change,
but the defiance remains the same. We throw up our hands
and say, "When am I ever going to outgrow this? When is
this no longer going to be a part of my life?" We are desperate to move on, but we can't. We have prayed about it and
talked about it, but it is still there. I call this "the usual defiance." It's really just another way of saying, "Different day,
same old problems." Can you relate to that? I know you can.

> As he was talking with them, Goliath, the Philistine
> champion from Gath, stepped out from his lines and
> shouted his *usual* defiance, and David heard it.
> —1 SAMUEL 17:23, NIV

I am not only the lead pastor at Real Life Church, but I
am also the administrator at Real Life Counseling Center,
where we provide free professional counseling to our community. In my role as a counselor one of the most common

78

phrases I hear goes something like this: "Well, you know. It's just the same old same old."

Is your "usual" keeping you from the life you envision? The usual comes into our lives in three ways: our provision, our pattern, and our persecutors. We will spend a day focusing on each one. All three have a unique way of sabotaging our lives. Plan to spend some time battling with the way you have always been. Since you're reading this book, there's a pretty good chance you're tired of at least one thing in your life and want to change it. That means you'll have to face the person in the mirror.

Our usual defiance is connected to provision. Too often in life when we face an obstacle, we feel as if we don't have the provision needed to get us past it. Our problems are not hard to identify. If we knew what to do to eliminate them, we would have taken the necessary measures. So instead of dealing with the problem and facing it, we end up building our lives around it. We can actually make provision for our problems instead of making provision to remove them. This will set us up for failure. The giant is only a giant when we give him what he needs to dominate us.

Maybe you struggle with a nicotine addiction and have tried many times in the past to stop smoking. But instead of suffering through the cravings and becoming healthier, you say things such as, "I need a cigarette to cope with my stressful life," or, "I have an addictive personality, so I can't help it." It is always easier to pass the buck than it is to accept the blame.

We should be evicting our misery, not building mansions for it.

Make no provision for the flesh to fulfill its lusts.

—ROMANS 13:14

It is very hard for me to drive by a doughnut shop without stopping. While this may seem trivial to you, when you are constantly battling with your weight, a doughnut shop can seem as big as Goliath! I love to eat pastries, and bear claws are definitely my weakness! Who knew bears were apple-filled? When driving to my office, I always take a route that does not include driving past the bakery. I resist my usual defiance.

I refuse to make provision for my flesh and set myself up to repeat the weight problems I battled in the past. I refuse to be the man driving past the local doughnut shop and as he approaches prays, "Dear Lord, if it's Your will for me to eat this unhealthy food today, let there be a parking spot available right at the front door." After circling the block for a half an hour, it finally became God's will!

You will never become the person you want to be by providing bullets for the gun your flesh will use to shoot you! The bakery is not the only place I cannot go. There are other locations that I know better than to visit. If I want to avoid the lion, I must stay out of his den. It could be that you're making provision for your flesh by what you choose to think or something as basic as laziness. Whatever the case, it's time for an eviction.

It's always easier when facing "the usual" to blame God, circumstances, or others rather than take the provision that has been given to us and do the work. Like the addict who has been given a good home, good family, new job, and support team but falls back into old patterns, instead of taking the provision and confronting themselves, they choose to self-destruct.

So now the question becomes: Will you do the hard work of confronting yourself or will you continue to allow your life to be dominated by "the usual"? God will provide for the future.

> In the desert the whole community grumbled against Moses and Aaron. The Israelites said to them, "If only we had died by the Lord's hand in Egypt! There we sat around pots of meat and ate all the food we wanted, but you have brought us out into this desert to starve this entire assembly to death." Then the Lord said to Moses, "I will rain down bread from heaven for you. The people are to go out each day and gather enough for that day. In this way I will test them and see whether they will follow my instructions...."
>
> When the dew was gone, thin flakes like frost on the ground appeared on the desert floor. When the Israelites saw it, they said to each other, "What is it?" For they did not know what it was. Moses said to them, "It is the bread the Lord has given you to eat. This is what the Lord has commanded: 'Everyone is to gather as much as they need. Take an omer for each person you have in your tent.'" The Israelites did as they were told; some gathered much, some little....
>
> The Israelites ate manna forty years, until they came to a land that was settled.
>
> —Exodus 16:2–4, 14–17, 35, niv

During their forty-year trek through the wilderness, the children of Israel often complained to God about being hungry. It was a "usual" topic. In the previous verses we find out God regularly provided manna for them to eat and all they had to do was go out and get it. It was their provision. Like clockwork, for forty years God provided the nourishment they needed.

God will give you what you need as well. When you get serious about finding your future, breaking free from your past, and establishing the new you, God will show up in the form of provision. God will always send manna. Just as God provided a star for the wise men to follow, God will provide you earthbound stars to help you get to where you want to go. He might put the right people in your life. He might arrange your circumstances so you can be in a new job or develop some new friendships. He might use the ministries of your church to give you what you need. I don't know exactly how He will do it, but God will provide.

Serious people always seem to have God's undivided attention. This book is part of your provision. As you move through each page, carefully consider what God is trying to say and provide for you.

Notice in the passage from Exodus 16 that even though God was providing, the Israelites still had work to do. They had to go out six days a week and gather their own manna. Yes, God provided it, but they had to gather it. Provision is not an excuse to be lazy.

Often people say to me, "I just wish it would get better"

or, "I just keep waiting and hoping, but nothing ever changes." My response to that is usually, "What are you doing while you're waiting? How are you contributing to what God wants to do in your life?"

Think about the Israelite sitting in his tent, staring at his empty jar. No matter how hard he wishes or hopes that it will miraculously fill up with manna, it's not going to happen because God said, "Gather your own manna." I guess the question I need to ask you is, Will you gather your own manna? Or will you be like the Israelite who stares at his empty jar and complains because his neighbors are all eating?

Your response might be, "Well, I would but I can't get out of bed to gather my own manna because I'm having a bad day" or, "I can't gather any manna because my neighbor takes everything close to my house and so it's his fault" or, "I can't gather manna because thirty years ago I twisted my ankle out gathering manna, and I just keep reliving the trauma of my past."

All that is separating you from the future you want are your excuses. When it comes to our "usual defiance," we are often tempted to get lazy because we are so used to it. When you get serious, God will provide everything you need to change, but you must gather the manna.

REFLECTION JOURNAL

What changes will you need to make in order to stop providing your flesh what it needs to sabotage your life?

_____

_____

_____

_____

_____

_____

_____

_____

_____

_____

_____

_____

_____

_____

_____

_____

_____

Day 14

YOU'RE SO PREDICTABLE

Challenge your routines today. Color outside the lines
and create situations that catch your devils off guard!

Key Verse: *Do not conform to the pattern of this world.*
—ROMANS 12:2, NIV

O FTEN OUR "USUAL defiance" is invited into our lives
because of the patterns we have established and
become accustomed to. It's our usual way of acting. Just as a
radar screen can track a hurricane spinning across the ocean
about to make landfall, our devils can usually track us based
upon our past behavior. We have become predictable.

A pattern is a regular, repetitive, predictable form, order, or
arrangement of behavior. This is what Moses received from
God in Exodus 24:17–18. In that passage he climbed up on a
mountain and met with God for forty days and forty nights.
During that time he received the plans, or pattern, that would
be used to build the Old Testament tabernacle. So for forty
days he was gathering information that would impact the
future. The Old Testament tabernacle was a big deal because
in those days that was where the presence of God dwelt.

God told Moses, "Then have them make a sanctuary for
me, and I will dwell among them. Make this tabernacle and
all its furnishings exactly like the pattern I will show you"
(Exod. 25:8–9, NIV).

In essence God was giving Moses a pattern and was

requesting that he follow the instructions. Like most of my male counterparts, I have never been very good at following instructions. This behavior has gotten the best of me on more than one occasion.

I remember one such case in which I was attempting to put together a swing set for my youngest son, Payte. Six hours into the project, I realized the instructions were included for a reason! Needless to say, I started over, this time with instructions in hand.

I encourage you to take the time to read Exodus 25–30 because you will see just how detailed the pattern really is. There are vivid descriptions of everything from the ark of the covenant to the colors on the walls.

Just as God gave Moses the pattern for the tabernacle, He will give you the pattern to build your new life. One of the reasons you need to hang in there and do this is because during your forty days God will help you and strengthen you a little more every day as you establish your new patterns.

The unwanted patterns we've established affect us physically, spiritually, and emotionally. While they may not necessarily be sinful, they are still classified as self-sabotage.

One of my favorite childhood memories is spending the long, lazy summer days with my Grandma Daisy. I can still feel the cool wind blowing through the tall elm trees in her front yard and can taste the mulberries that grew just past her broken-down fence. Her big, two-story house is a place I often visit in my memories.

Grandma Daisy was an avid quilter and took great

pleasure in teaching her grandsons to sew. She knew there was just something about a man who could sew on a button that women couldn't resist! She would say to me, "Son, if you get the pattern right, the rest will be easy." From my grandmother, I learned that the most important thing wasn't to think about the entire quilt but to concentrate on the pattern, because if I got the pattern wrong, the quilt would be ruined.

There are patterns in life too. That's why the Bible tells us, "Do not conform to the pattern of this world" (Rom. 12:2, NIV). Following the wrong pattern ruins lives too, not just quilts.

Whatever your old patterns are, whatever your "usual defiance" looks like, now is the time to establish the new. But first you have to make up your mind that you are no longer going to conform to the usual, predictable patterns of your past.

To conform means to behave in an expected way. Whatever you usually do to sabotage your life, you must make up your mind to follow a different pattern.

This is going to take an extraordinary amount of work and will take your full cooperation. It will feel uncomfortable at first, and you may even feel as if you're not being yourself. Jesus taught that the only way to find new life is to lose the one we have. The life you are living is no doubt full of patterns that need to be changed. Identifying and changing those patterns is crucial as you continue in your forty-day challenge.

REFLECTION JOURNAL

Think about your negative patterns of behavior. Ask yourself:
Where am I when I participate in them? Who am I with?
What am I doing?

_____

_____

_____

_____

_____

_____

_____

_____

_____

_____

_____

_____

_____

_____

_____

_____

_____

Day 15

ARE YOU TALKING TO ME?

Expect the Devil to get personal today. He might want to talk about things that you would just as soon forget. Make it a conversation that he will regret!

Key Verse: *David said to the Philistine, "You come against me with sword and spear and javelin, but I come against you in the name of the LORD Almighty, the God of the armies of Israel, whom you have defied."*
—1 SAMUEL 17:45, NIV

OUR USUAL DEFIANCE often takes the form of persecution. Persecutors come into our lives in various ways: people, problems, and circumstances are the normal culprits. In many cases we feel as if the odds are stacked against us, and we sometimes say things such as, "What's the use anyway?" Our devils antagonize and we listen.

David's persecutor was doing a lot of talking:

When the Philistine looked and saw David, he despised him. For he was a youth and ruddy with a handsome appearance. The Philistine said to David, "Am I a dog, that you come to me with sticks?" Then the Philistine cursed David by his gods.
—1 SAMUEL 17:42–43

As David listened, maybe he thought, "Stick and stones can break my bones, but names can never hurt me." Of course we know that's never the case. Goliath's taunts were insulting and personal. He took aim at David's king, family, God, and appearance. Nothing was off limits to Goliath. David's feelings would not be spared.

You, no doubt, have had similar days, times when your persecutor cuts you to the core. Goliath knew exactly what to say to get a response out of David. This would prove to be a fatal mistake for Goliath. Unfortunately we rarely respond the way David did. Instead of taking aim at our giants, we want to run, hide, and give in to the devils that are hot on our trail.

In order for you to defeat the "usual," at some point you have to look past the odds, past the way things have always been, past your critics, and fight your battles head-on. Be a nonconformist!

David was such a man.

David's persecutor was a person—a giant. He was a fierce warrior whose armor probably weighed more than David did. This champion from Gath stood over nine feet tall and would, no doubt, even make Chuck Norris a little nervous! (See 1 Samuel 17:1–16.)

Not even Walker, Texas Ranger could have handled this problem in a sixty-minute episode! This giant was much more than just a man; he represented everything that was standing in David's way.

Goliath taunted Israel for forty days before David finally had enough and took aim with his slingshot and stones. Forty is a number of opposition. During the forty days Goliath taunted the Israelites, David had a decision to make. It's the same decision that you must make: *Are you going to conform and have what you have always had? Or are you going to stand toe to toe with your opposition and be defiant right back?*

Goliath represented much more than just a giant-size fight. He wasn't only in Israel's way, keeping them from victory over the Philistines. He was also blocking the path to the life David had only imagined as he spent his days tending his father's sheep. Yes, the giant spoke. David couldn't prevent him from talking. But it would be Goliath's last conversation because instead of agreeing with Goliath, David took aim. Grab some stones and do the same.

REFLECTION JOURNAL

What does your devil usually whisper about the future? During your journaling time, write a response letter but this time see yourself as David.

_____

_____

_____

_____

_____

_____

_____

_____

_____

_____

_____

_____

Real People, Real Stories

Paula's Story

Paula, a longtime follower of Christ, was no stranger to the wiles of the Devil. She, however, never dreamed of treating overeating as an enemy. But after struggling with her weight for years, Paula decided to use her forty-day challenge to rethink how she approached weight loss. Having tried every diet program and pill available, she had all but given up hope.

Paula soon realized she had to get to the root and address her problem with overeating. "I never saw my weight as a spiritual issue until then," she said. "Something had to be done about the lack of ability to control my flesh."

For the first time in her life, Paula prayed and asked God to help her fight the devil of overeating. "I was afraid to pray for weight loss before," she said. "I saw it as selfishness. After all, there are so many greater needs out there than the size of my pants."

Paula began her forty-day challenge with apprehensiveness. This approach was totally foreign to her. However, something quickly changed. Paula's appetite started getting smaller, and she no longer felt compelled to eat between meals. Before she knew it, the weight was coming off. At the time I interviewed her, Paula was well past the forty-day mark. She is still approaching weight loss as a spiritual issue and continues to move closer to her goal weight. Paula told me, "I now realize that this devil has no power over me, other than the power I give to it."

PART V

DEFIANCE ON A DAILY BASIS

For forty days the Philistine came forward every morning and evening and took his stand.

—1 SAMUEL 17:16, NIV

I am grateful for all my problems. After each one was overcome, I became stronger and more able to meet those that were still to come. I grew in all my difficulties.[1]

—J. C. PENNEY

Day 16
YOU CAN'T OUTRUN A GIANT

Running from a giant will only get you speared
in the back. Like an oversized shadow, your
giant will be in pursuit. Today show him what
happens when he catches up to a king!

Key Verse: *David left his things with the keeper
of the equipment, and he ran to the battle line.*
—1 SAMUEL 17:22

WHEN I READ the story of David and Goliath, I picture David as a skinny, red-faced boy with a bag full of rocks, like the kind I would skip at the creek on Saturday when I was a kid. There was David, standing between two armies, just a few feet away from a drooling, cursing monster. The chances of him defeating Goliath were slim to none. But what Goliath didn't know was that in the chest of this freckled-faced kid beat the heart of a king.

Samuel said to Jesse, "Are these all your young men?"
And he said, "There remains yet the youngest, and there
he is shepherding the flock." Then Samuel said to Jesse,
"Send and bring him, for we will not sit down until he
comes here." So he sent and brought him in.... And
the LORD said, "Arise, anoint him, for this is he." Then
Samuel took the horn of oil, and anointed him in the
midst of his brothers. And the Spirit of the LORD came
on David from that day forward.
—1 SAMUEL 16:11–13

Goliath did not realize who he was fighting. He didn't realize he was in the presence of royalty. Understand that you have that same heart as David did. You don't have to cower in fear when facing your opposition for one day or forty days, because you are royalty. You are a child of the King of kings!

Just as it was with David, your opposition may not see the royal heart beating in your chest. Your peers may not see it, and even your family may not be aware of it. But I can assure you that you have a king's heart.

Everyone at Jesse's house the day David was anointed king looked at physical appearance, including the prophet Samuel. But God was looking at the heart.

Yes, the enemy has his champions, and I am sure they have created chaos in your life, but the secret to winning any battle is seeing yourself as a champion and believing in yourself enough to fight the monster.

Your Goliath is probably not from Gath. Your giant probably looks more like rejection, insecurity, fear, depression, financial calamity, health problems, loneliness, and abuse.

Your giant doesn't wear armor; your giant wears you!

David's opposition had two feet, and he could follow David wherever he chose to go. Some people think all they need to have a better future is to move to a different environment. They believe that if they get a fresh start, their opposition will somehow just go away. Some even think getting divorced and finding someone new will fix their unhappiness. The problem with that theory is that, as it was with David, your opposition goes where you go. It eats at all your favorite restaurants. It sleeps comfortably in your bed. This means you must face your opposition on the inside rather than run from it on the outside. If you don't fix what you are struggling with on the inside, the struggle will follow you from place to place.

A few years ago I received a phone call from a friend who was facing some personal demons. He said, "I think my family and I will move to your city to get a fresh start. I just think I need a change of scenery." I told him, "If you can't do the right thing where you are, you won't be able to do the right thing where you're going."

Instead of running from our opposition, we must face it and defeat it! A change of environment will never satisfy until the heart is changed.

REFLECTION JOURNAL

Are you running from your opposition instead of facing it? How will you change this?

_____

_____

_____

_____

_____

_____

_____

_____

Day 17

SAUL HEARD A GIANT; DAVID HEARD GOD

Goliath looked far more intimidating than he
actually was. Everyone was saying, "He is so big.
How can David hit him?" David was saying, "He is
so big, how can I miss him?" Today focus on the
size of God rather than the size of the giant.

Key Verse: *Who is this uncircumcised Philistine
that he should defy the armies of the living God?*
—1 SAMUEL 17:26

GOLIATH'S BOOMING VOICE carried his taunts across
the valley: "Why do you even bother to line up for
battle? Why do you even choose to fight when you know
you can't win?" When the men of Israel heard his words,
"they were filled with terror" (1 Sam. 17:11).

Goliath was doing more than questioning David's ability
with his jabs. He was questioning God's ability.

Do you recognize that voice? Does the enemy say to you,
"Why even bother, you big idiot? You are outmatched and
overpowered. Not even God can help you."

For most people, that voice says things such as: "You have
never been able to exercise and lose weight." "You're always
going to be depressed because you're just like your mom."
"You can't be happy like everyone else because you're a victim."
"You need this habit to help you with all the stress in your life."

Are you, like King Saul, terrified to fight your own battles because the voice of the opposition has left you believing you can't win?

I think it is important to note that of all the men standing before Goliath, King Saul was the most qualified to fight Goliath. The Bible says Saul was "as handsome a young man as could be found anywhere in Israel, and he was a head taller than anyone else" (1 Sam. 9:2, NIV).

As noted earlier, even Samuel, the most respected and honest priest of his time, got caught up in appearances. As Jesse's three oldest sons passed by, all Samuel noticed were their broad shoulders and rippling biceps—the kind that would fit perfectly into a king's armor. Just like the nation of Israel, even Samuel wanted a king who looked like a champion.

Saul was the logical choice to fight the giant that day. He was bigger than any other man under his command and he certainly towered over the shepherd boy from Bethlehem. We know this because the Bible tells us Saul's armor didn't fit David (1 Sam. 17:38–39).

David must have looked like a kindergartener trying on one of his dad's work uniforms. It no doubt swallowed him up. The man who could wear this armor would be more of a challenge for Goliath than a boy who came to the battle just to bring cheese to his older brothers.

King Saul, no doubt, was the second-tallest man on the battlefield that day, but because of the voice of the opposition he was terrified and dismayed. Saul had all the potential, charisma, and size needed for winning battles. He even had a fan club cheering him on; however, he was content to sit back while the enemy dominated his life. David, however, would not tolerate such defiance.

Saul may have been bigger on the outside, but David was the bigger man.

This is a picture of our lives in many cases. Even though we have the armor of God protecting us, the Word as our sword, faith as our shield, and the Holy Spirit guiding us, we choose to allow the voice of the enemy to keep us from fighting battles that are in our power to win.

Saul heard the voice of the enemy. David heard the voice of God. Whose voice will you choose to hear?

> Now the Philistines gathered their forces for war....For forty days the Philistine came forward every morning and evening and took his stand....As he was talking with them, Goliath, the Philistine champion from Gath, stepped out from his lines and shouted his usual defiance, and David heard it.
> —1 Samuel 17:1, 16, 23, niv

This particular battle was unlike most battles fought during this time period, because it went on for forty days. It was defiance on a daily basis.

If you're reading this book to discover how to change your life, I'd bet this is probably a picture of your life. It's an everyday struggle with a familiar enemy. Most of us lose the battle before it ever begins, because battles are bloody, painful, and tedious. Daily defiance is exhausting!

In this particular battle Goliath was there every

morning and every evening. That tells me he was there when they got up and when they went to bed.

Does that sound familiar? You wake up and your opposition is there; you go to bed and your opposition is still there. Goliath was constantly in their faces, flaunting his strength before the seemingly helpless army of King Saul. I imagine King Saul slept with one eye open, because no matter how hard he tried to change the channel in his mind, his thoughts kept going back to the monster in the valley.

Is this happening in your life right now? Are you ever aware of the enemy's champion as he brazenly walks through every waking thought you have? Is he using the same old stuff he has been using on you for weeks, months, and years? Is it just "the usual"?

Unfortunately for a lot of us Goliath is nothing new. We are well-acquainted with him. He doesn't bother with a disguise because he knows that what has worked on us in the past will continue to work on us in the future. That is, until now!

I have gone through seasons in my life where, until I decided to fight my battle, my giant was there with me every second of every day. There have been seasons in my life when I got up with, ate breakfast with, rode to work with, spent the day with, came home with, and went to bed with my giant.

Defiance on a daily basis is one of the most exhausting, debilitating, and depressing things imaginable. If you don't rise up and confront the giant, the usual defiance will keep you from winning the battle.

Now the Israelites had been saying, "Do you see how
this man keeps coming out?"
—1 Samuel 17:25, NIV

Goliath kept coming. He never took a vacation day or
decided to just not show up. He had taken his stand and
somebody was going to win. That winner can be you if
you'll do like David did and focus on the size of your God
instead of on the size of your goliath.

REFLECTION JOURNAL

*Think about those familiar enemies, the ones that are there
when you wake up and when you lie down. As David did, will
you choose to focus on the size of your God rather than focus on
the size of your giant?*

_____

_____

_____

_____

_____

_____

_____

_____

_____

_____

_____

Day 18

IT'S TIME TO DEFY
YOUR DEFIANCE

The last thing Goliath expected was to see David running toward him. Usually his opponents were running in the opposite direction. Meet your opposition head-on today. Don't be friendly!

Key Verse: *As the Philistine moved closer to attack him, David ran quickly toward the battle line to meet him.*
—1 Samuel 17:48, NIV

W ILL YOU TURN the tables on the enemy and do the unexpected? Will you rush the giant? Will you do the unusual and attack your usual?

That's what David did.

As the Philistine moved closer to attack him, David ran quickly toward the battle line to meet him. Reaching into his bag and taking out a stone, he slung it and struck the Philistine on the forehead. The stone sank into his forehead, and he fell facedown on the ground. So David triumphed over the Philistine with a sling and a stone; without a sword in his hand he struck down the Philistine and killed him.

—1 Samuel 17:48–50, NIV

Lest we overlook an important point because it is so obvious, let me remind you, *David had never killed a giant before.* If you are going to have what you've never had, you're going to have to do what you've never done. You need to walk into the battle in your mind before you walk there in your shoes.

I am sure the scenario played over and over in the head of the boy from Bethlehem: "Rush the giant, put the rock in the slingshot, and make the kill!" I can hear David talking to himself and preparing for victory, saying things such as, "You can do this! You have killed lions and bears! God is with you!"

David no doubt replayed the day in his mind when Samuel visited his home, passed over all his brothers, and anointed him as king. Perhaps he remembered the smell of the oil as it ran down his face, and he thought to himself, "A king could kill a giant."

I can imagine him picking up the rock he would use as a missile to bring down the menacing monster and thinking, "This is perfect for giant slaying."

Don't let David be the only giant slayer you know of. *It's time to defy your defiance!*

Let's try an experiment with 1 Samuel 17:16. Replace "the Philistine" with your name, so it would read like this: "For forty days (your name here) came forward every morning and every evening and took his stand!"

Wow, that's a game changer! What if you became as threatening to your giant as your giant has been to you?

We read in 1 Samuel 17:40 that David "took his staff in his hand, chose five smooth stones from the stream, put them in the pouch of his shepherd's bag and, with his sling in his hand, approached the Philistine" (NIV).

It has always been interesting to me that David chose five smooth stones when he would need only one to kill Goliath. Four of the five were placed in what the Bible calls a shepherd's bag. Bags comparable to this one are still used by shepherds today in similar cultures. They are primarily used to carry provisions for the future such as food and water.

It was no accident that David placed extra rocks in the bag he so often depended upon for his future needs. David wasn't going to spend his life celebrating the slaying of one giant. No, by picking up five stones instead of one, he was ensuring that his future victories would be greater than his past successes. Goliath had others in his family David had not yet had the pleasure of meeting! Before David killed Goliath he was planning on killing the whole family. Giant killers take no prisoners.

> These four were descendants of Rapha in Gath, and they
> fell at the hands of David and his men.
> —2 Samuel 21:22, NIV

Always keep extra rocks on hand, because you never know when you might meet a giant and his family. King David had many victories, but he had some rough days as well. He stood face-to-face with Goliath, but he also stood face-to-face with Bathsheba. He felt the breath of the champion from Gath on his face as Goliath swore and cursed the God of Israel, but David also felt the warm breath of his mistress. He slaughtered the enemy but lost the battle with his own selfish desires. Like you, King David was not a perfect man, but he did learn from his past mistakes, and as a result, his future changed.

> So David slept with his fathers and was buried in the City of David. David reigned over Israel forty years. He reigned seven years in Hebron and thirty-three years in Jerusalem.
>
> —1 Kings 2:10–11

This verse gives us a summary of King David's life and rule over Israel. Once again we find the number forty and the biblical precedence continues to be set before us. Goliath was down in the valley calling out for forty days and because David did the right thing, kept the right perspective, and chose to see the size of his God over the size of his opponent, it changed the course of his life over the next forty years. David had some bumps along the way, but he finished strong, because he believed that no matter what today looked like, tomorrow would be better. Yesterday held David's failure; tomorrow held David's future.

As you continue in this challenge, you are going to be confronted with, the "usual defiance." It will not be a surprise attack. It will be a familiar attack. Kill the familiar!

David's decision to defy his defiance changed everything.

> The men of Israel said, "…it will be that the man who kills him, the king will enrich him with great riches, will give him his daughter, and will make his father's house exempt from taxes in Israel."
>
> —1 Samuel 17:25

King Saul promised to give great wealth to whoever killed Goliath, to give the man his daughter in marriage, and to exempt the victor's family from paying taxes (1 Sam. 17:25). The king made good on that promise. After Goliath was dead, David married the king's daughter and received great wealth and a high rank in the king's army, and his family was exempt from taxes! David literally won the lottery. He went from living in the field to living in the finest house in the land. He went from serenading sheep to serenading the king.

All those things happened because he decided to defy his defiance. Just think about how different things might have looked if David had chosen not to fight that day. There would have been no princess, no job, no new house, and no future. David would have gone back to a shepherd's life, and his rise to the throne would have been compromised.

Like David, you must decide to face your opposition. *You were created to do more than sing to sheep. You were created to play for the King!*

The prophet Joel described life as "a valley of decision" (Joel 3:14). Every day is all about making the right choices. We don't always get to choose everything that happens to us. We don't get to decide when or where Goliath might show up. We do, however, determine how we will respond to our usual defiance, and that decision will determine where our lives will go.

REFLECTION JOURNAL

What usually keeps you from running toward the usual? How will you do the unexpected and rush the giant?

_____

_____

_____

_____

_____

_____

_____

_____

_____

_____

_____

_____

_____

_____

_____

_____

_____

Day 19

DO YOU HAVE AN "EXCEPT"?

Expect the skeletons in your closet to spill out
today. Like David, decide to no longer give them
power in your life. Remember, the Devil's agenda
is to keep you so focused on where you have been
that you forget about where you are going.

Key Verse: *For David had done what was right
in the eyes of the LORD and had not failed to keep
any of the LORD's commands all the days of his
life*—except *in the case of Uriah the Hittite.*

—1 KINGS 15:5, NIV, EMPHASIS ADDED

DAVID'S BIGGEST GIANT wasn't Goliath.

After David stood over the headless body of
Goliath, this man after God's own heart would eventually
break two commandments. He slept with another man's
wife and then had her husband murdered. David could
have decided his life was over, resigned the throne, and
moved into seclusion, but instead he corrected his behavior.

Part of your forty-day journey will include coming to
terms with where you have been so you can get to where
you want to be. David's next giant would be the man in the
mirror. As today's key verse states, David had done what
was right in the Lord's sight all the days of his life, *except* in
the case of Uriah the Hittite.

We all have an "except." We all have something from our
past that could be used as an excuse to settle for a future

that is far less than we want. Maybe your "except" is like that of a friend of mine, who committed a murder but now pastors one of the largest churches in America. David's "except" was adultery and murder. No matter how we have behaved in the past, like David, we must do what is right in the eyes of the Lord and get back on track.

David did not accept his except! What about you? Have you accepted your except? Have you decided that you can never have a good future because of something that occurred in the past? Perhaps you haven't yet come to terms with your "except," and as a result you can't move past it.

David's adultery and killing of Bathsheba's husband was unacceptable. However, David knew the secret to not allowing his past to define him.

When the prophet Nathan cornered David about the matter, David was caught. However, it wasn't the exposure of David's sin that allowed him to move on and enjoy a great future. It was his willingness to see his behavior for what it was and make the needed adjustments.

The sins of your past may or may not be known. As far as we know, Nathan never exposed David to the nation of Israel nor did he post what David had done on Facebook. The lesson in this story is that David saw his past behavior as unacceptable and changed.

Once David saw his sin for what it was, he realized the future was at stake. As a result, David refused to allow his "except" to define him.

No doubt your past, like mine, is full of exceptions. Perhaps you have brought some of these "exceptions" upon yourself while others have been inflicted upon you. Whatever the case, it's important that you identify your exceptions and decide to no longer accept them. You will never find your future if you are still allowing the mistakes of your past to define you.

Listen to David as he refuses to accept his except.

> Have mercy on me, O God, according to Your loving-kindness; according to the abundance of Your compassion, blot out my transgressions. Wash me thoroughly from my iniquity, and cleanse me from my sin. For I acknowledge my transgressions, and my sin is ever before me. Against You, You only, have I sinned, and done this evil in Your sight, so that You are justified when You speak, and You are blameless when You judge. I was brought forth in iniquity, and in sin my mother conceived me. You desire truth in the inward parts, and in the hidden part You make me to know wisdom. Purify me with hyssop, and I will be clean; wash me, and I will be whiter than snow.
>
> —PSALM 51:1–7

There is no mention of Bathsheba and the affair, no mention of Uriah and the political need to cover up his brutal murder in this prayer. No mention of David's rights. No mention of excuses. David does not bring up his dysfunctional family or the rejection he felt as a boy. It's just David facing his devil. David never mentions the outward circumstances of his past. He does, however, on two occasions talk about his desire for truth on the inside.

Today decide to look at your past failures honestly and face them head-on. Decide not to accept your except!

REFLECTION JOURNAL

Have you allowed the mistakes of your past to keep you from facing your personal devils? Have you decided that your "except" is too big for God to handle?

_____

_____

_____

_____

_____

_____

_____

_____

_____

_____

_____

_____

_____

Real People, Real Stories

Shara's Story

Shara's forty-day challenge was a little unusual. She, like so many others, felt the need to confront an area of her life that we would not classify as sin. In fact, the devil she chose to face is a regular occurrence in the lives of many people. Yet her devil was slowly taking over her life and robbing her of precious time that she should have been spending with her children.

This is what Shara had to say about her devil: "I could not stop thinking about it. My mind was constantly going there. It had slowly grown to the point to where it had taken over every aspect of my life. I used my forty-day challenge to confront my Facebook addiction."

Shara explained to me that she was a stay-at-home mom and Facebook often gave her the adult conversation she yearned for. However, it wasn't long until she found herself constantly stopping to check her phone for new notifications. Facebook was taking over her life. As a result, she felt rushed and always pressed for time.

The forty-day challenge gave her the motivation and strength she needed to face her devil. She started deciding to not be on Facebook as often. While this may seem like an easy task, for her it was very difficult. Eventually she began putting her phone away in the morning and not checking it until the end of the day. By the end of the forty days, she had gone an entire week without checking Facebook. For her, this was a huge accomplishment.

"Confronting my Facebook addition not only took away a lot of unnecessary stress, but it also gave me more time to spend with my little ones," she said. "Now Facebook is something that enhances my life, not rules my life."

PART VI

MISSION: IMPOSSIBLE

And he said to Him, "O my Lord, how can I save Israel? Indeed my clan is the weakest in Manasseh, and I am the youngest in my father's house." Then the LORD said to him, "But I will be with you, and you will strike the Midianites as one man."

—JUDGES 6:15–16

The Midianites were humbled before the children of Israel and did not lift their heads high again. The land had peace for forty years in the days of Gideon.

—JUDGES 8:28

The only place where your dream becomes impossible is in your own thinking.[1]

—ROBERT H. SCHULLER

Day 20

THIS IS IMPOSSIBLE

Maybe you are struggling a little today. Relax, it's OK. Remember, you bought this book for a reason. Today just be willing to keep going.

Key Verse: *And he said to Him, "O my Lord, how can I save Israel? Indeed my clan is the weakest in Manasseh, and I am the youngest in my father's house." Then the LORD said to him, "But I will be with you, and you will strike the Midianites as one man."*
—JUDGES 6:15

E VERYONE LOVES AN underdog, right? They're the people who somehow manage to conquer insurmountable odds with little more than heart and determination. It's the underdog who lives on in the pages of history, not the person who had great ability but lacked determination.

I will be the first to admit that I always root for the person who is not supposed to win. You know, the one with the odds stacked against him, the dark horse no one sees coming until he's standing in the winner's circle.

I am not the only one who roots for the underdog, so does God.

When the angel of the LORD appeared to Gideon, he said, "The LORD is with you, mighty warrior."
—JUDGES 6:12, NIV

That statement must have seemed like a slap in the face to the runt from Manasseh. After all, his clan was weak and his family was among the least. "Mighty warrior" must have seemed like a rotten joke. Mighty *mouse* would have been more appropriate.

Gideon may not have seen himself as mighty, but God was about to issue a challenge to him—one that would force Gideon to first look inside himself. The challenge was simple: face the enemy.

Except for creation, anytime God does something big on Earth, He does it in partnership with people. God even partnered with a person in His plan of redemption, causing Jesus to be born of a virgin and live among humanity for thirty-three years. God stands ready to partner with you as you strive to overcome the destructive behaviors of your past. Underdogs can become overcomers once God is involved.

When it comes to finding our future by facing our opposition, we often have the willingness but not the ability. We feel under-qualified, unequal to the daunting task ahead of us. Such was the case with Gideon. As we read in our key verse, he simply did not believe he had what it would take.

Gideon did not start off with ability. He started only with willingness. Well, first skepticism, then willingness. When you think of your personal devils, you may feel as if you do not have the ability either. Like Gideon, you might even be reminded of the weakness in your family. This can be especially true if you come from a long line of addicts or if your family tree is full of nuts! Don't worry about it!

You provide the willingness and allow God to provide the ability. He is your partner.

Gideon's story probably has a familiar ring to it. The enemy was overwhelming and life was underwhelming. Like locusts, the enemy regularly came to devour any hope of Gideon having a future beyond mediocrity and derision. Gideon and his family were reduced to hiding instead of fighting. At one point survival became more important than success (Judg. 6:1–5).

To win an impossible battle, always begin by tipping the scales in your favor. When Israel was made weak before their enemy the Midianites, they cried out to the Lord for help (Judg. 6:6). Your greatest concern should never be who or what is fighting against you but, rather, who is fighting beside you.

The scales would tip in Israel's favor after they cried out to God. For seven years Israel had opened themselves up to attack by removing God from the equation.

> The children of Israel did evil in the sight of the LORD, so the LORD gave them into the hands of Midian for seven years. The hands of Midian dominated Israel, and because of Midian the children of Israel made hiding places for themselves in the mountains, caves, and strongholds.
>
> —JUDGES 6:1–2

Now, after years of struggle and exhaustion, they were finally ready to fight back, but first it would require a shift in their lifestyle.

Are you ready to fight back? Are you ready to tip the

scales in your favor? That begins by including God in the battle and crying out for His help.

REFLECTION JOURNAL

Do you feel like an underdog, as if the deck is stacked against you? Describe why you feel that way and commit to moving forward despite your handicap.

_____

_____

_____

_____

_____

_____

_____

_____

_____

_____

_____

_____

_____

_____

_____

Day 21

IMPOSSIBLE BATTLES
REQUIRE PROPER ALTARS

Expect your spiritual condition to be challenged
today. Be honest with yourself and with God about
the condition of your altar. Rebuild if necessary!

Key Verse: *Tear down your father's altar to Baal and cut
down the Asherah pole beside it. Then build a proper kind
of altar to the* LORD *your God on the top of this height.*
—JUDGES 6:25–26, NIV

I T IS NO accident that before Gideon met the enemy, he
first met with God.

> That same night the LORD said to him, "Take the second
> bull from your father's herd, the one seven years old.
> Tear down your father's altar to Baal and cut down the
> Asherah pole beside it. Then build a proper kind of altar
> to the LORD your God on the top of this height. Using
> the wood of the Asherah pole that you cut down, offer
> the second bull as a burnt offering."
> —JUDGES 6:25–26, NIV

Normal practice was to offer God the first of everything,
but this time God asked for the second. The second bull
was seven years old. One year of life was to be offered for
each of the seven years Israel had lived with a faulty altar.

In addition Baal had to be removed and a proper kind of altar established.

Now that you are halfway through this challenge, have you considered checking the condition of your altar? Consider those areas of your life that you have placed on Baal's altar, those areas that are broken down not because of the enemy but because of God's absence. The size of Gideon's enemy was never the real problem. The real problem was the condition of Israel's altar. Without God's partnership, you simply will not win.

I realize that if you are reading this book, there is a good chance that you, like Gideon, are overwhelmed by a seemingly indestructible enemy. Like Rocky Balboa, you stare at the conditioned body of Apollo Creed and think to yourself, "Maybe everyone is right. Maybe this is a fight I cannot win." It doesn't have to be that way.

It wasn't always a life of hiding and constant invasion by the enemy for Gideon and his family. In fact, before Baal's altar was built, life was good. Just one chapter before the story of Gideon, in Judges chapter 5, Israel's leader Deborah cried out to God, saying:

> "May all Your enemies perish like this, O LORD! But may those who love Him rise like the sun when it rises in full strength." Then the land was at peace for forty years.
>
> —JUDGES 5:31

This verse predates the invasion of the Midianites and gives us a glimpse into Gideon's past. And once again we see the number forty and its connection to strength and peace.

I love the Lord of the Ring books. The loyalty shared between Frodo and his mismatched band of genuine friends warms my heart. I have read the series more than once, but you can't fully understand the books until you have read *The Hobbit*, which was written first. In much the same way, Judges 5:31 is a prequel to Gideon's story. It paints a very different picture of Israel than we read in Judges 6. Those who were now cave dwellers were once rays of sunshine.

In Judges 5 the number forty is connected to a life of blessing that was altered when someone built the wrong altar. In this story it was Gideon's father who had built an altar to Baal. In your story, no doubt, others have played a starring role in your lost battles. However, like Gideon you are responsible for building your own altar.

An overcomer can become an underdog in a relatively short amount of time when the training stops. Was there a time in your life when it seemed as if there was nothing you could not face, a time when you felt like the heavy-weight champion of your world but now you don't even feel like a contender?

Gideon's family had the same problem. Forty years of peace had quickly turned into seven years of misery. But that misery would come to an end when they built a proper altar. The same will happen to you.

REFLECTION JOURNAL

Is it possible that you are losing the battle with your flesh because you have removed God from that area of your life? Explain.

_____

_____

_____

_____

_____

_____

_____

_____

_____

_____

_____

_____

_____

_____

_____

_____

_____

_____

_____

Day 22

ALWAYS GO IN THE STRENGTH YOU HAVE

You can't do anything about the strength you don't
have. All you can do is start with the strength
you do have. Even if your strength is small, show
up. God has something up His sleeve today!

Key Verse: *The LORD turned to him and
said, "Go in the strength you have and save Israel
out of Midian's hand. Am I not sending you?"*

—JUDGES 6:14, NIV

IN JUDGES 6:14 God was essentially telling Gideon, "I
know you don't have much strength, but if you will go in
the strength that you do have, I will provide the rest of the
muscle to get the job done."

When God was calling Gideon into a life no longer
dominated by his enemy, God had a plan. Gideon, however, was not yet aware of God's plan. While Gideon was in
the winepress hiding from the Midianites, he did not know
that God would give him victory over a vast army with only
the help of three hundred men. Gideon had no idea that
the only weapon needed to slay the enemy would simply
be showing up at the battle site. (See Judges 7:15–23.) The
enemy would turn on each other and the battle would be
won, but it would all start with Gideon's decision to simply
go in the strength he had.

Again, God is showing us the power of His partnership.

No doubt some of you are staring down an addiction that seems the size of Mount Everest while others are thinking about the last few years and can see only havoc, hiding, and hopelessness. Remember, God has a plan that is unknown to you but is known to Him. He is not nervous about the outcome of the battle. His only concern is you. Keep in mind that God already knows the level of your strength. Your feelings of inadequacy never catch God off guard. He is aware.

He isn't asking you to find a way to get more strength before you begin the fight. No, His request is simple, "Go in the strength you have."

Sometimes we think, "Maybe after the next revival at our church, I will feel more empowered. Or maybe after I finish reading my Bible through in a year, I will be strong enough to face my devils." God didn't tell Gideon he needed more training. He just said, "Go."

Just as God had already mapped out Gideon's route to success, He has already made your map. Gideon started with thirty-two thousand warriors, but God said, "You have too many men for me to deliver Midian into their hands. I don't want Israel to boast and think they did this in their own strength."

Gideon stood in front of his army and said, "If anyone is afraid, you can leave." Twenty-two thousand men left that day. Still there were too many, so God instructed Gideon to take them down to the water so He could watch them drink.

But the LORD said to Gideon, "There are still too many people. Bring them down to the water, and I will test them for you there. When I say to you, 'This one will go with you,' he will go with you. Everyone about whom I will say, 'This one will not go with you,' will not go."

So he brought the people down to the water, and the LORD said to Gideon, "You shall set apart by himself everyone who laps the water with his tongue like dogs; likewise, everyone who kneels down to drink." The number of those who lapped, putting their hands to their mouths, was three hundred. The rest of the people had knelt to drink water.

The LORD said to Gideon, "With three hundred men who lapped to drink, I will save you and give the Midianites into your hands. All the rest of the people should go home."

—JUDGES 7:4–7

Here we see God's unknown plan. God's unknown plan always begins with the decision to "go in the strength you have." Leave the unknown up to God. Let Him worry about the impossible.

Gideon didn't win because his army was superior. Gideon won because he was willing to show up at the battle sight and see what God had up His sleeve. When you "go in the strength you have," God will show up for you too.

REFLECTION JOURNAL

Consider the strengths you have. What are they?

_____

_____

_____

_____

_____

_____

_____

_____

_____

_____

_____

_____

_____

_____

_____

_____

_____

_____

_____

_____

Day 23

BE THE DEVIL'S
WORST NIGHTMARE

What if the Devil stayed up at night drinking coffee
and refusing to lie down all because he was afraid you
might star in one of his dreams? Be a nightmare!

Key Verse: *The Midianites were humbled before the
children of Israel and did not lift their heads high again.
The land had peace for forty years in the days of Gideon.*

—JUDGES 8:28

HAVE YOU EVER been in the middle of a terrifying
dream, but you couldn't make yourself wake up?
Maybe you're being chased by a T-Rex or you're falling out
of an airplane. You are telling yourself, "Wake up, wake up,
this is not real," but it's like you are stuck in an impossible
situation. Finally you wake up covered in sweat and your
terror turns into relief as you realize it was only a dream.

What if you could turn that around, put the Devil in
that same situation, and be the one creating havoc for him?
What if you gave the Devil nightmares and made him wish
he could wake up to escape you? How does that sound?

That's what happened to Gideon.

Gideon came [into the Midianite camp] and overheard one
man who was telling his dream to another. The man said,
"Listen to a dream I had. I saw a dry cake of barley bread

126

rolling into the Midianite camp. It rolled up to a tent and struck it. It fell, turned upside down, and collapsed."

The other man responded, "This is none other than the sword of Gideon son of Joash the Israelite. God has given Midian and the whole camp into his hands."

—Judges 7:13–14

Gideon, the underdog and least qualified, was giving his devil nightmares. In this dream a barley loaf tumbles into the Devil's living room and causes destruction.

You might be thinking, "A barley loaf? How terrifying!" The fact that the man dreamed of this particular type of bread is no accident. This was not a loaf of Wonder Bread from Walmart. Nor was it a fresh-baked loaf from the local pastry shop. It was barley bread. Barley was considered inferior grain and half the value of wheat. This dream was prophesying that the inferior was about to destroy an enemy that had proven to be superior in the past.

The barley bread was Gideon and the barley bread can also be you. What Gideon lacked in ability, he would eventually more than make up for in willingness.

Perhaps you've heard the song "The Enemy's Camp." It was made popular in churches in the early nineties. In the verse the singer says he went into the enemy's camp and took what was stolen from him. There is no mention of an army. No mention of angels with flaming swords drawn. Just a lone Christian soldier in the camp of his adversary gathering up what is rightfully his. Thousands sang this song, jumping up and down and declaring Satan to be under their feet, only to return home and find out that they were still very much under his. *Victory over your devil is not simply a proclamation; it is a decision to act.*

Hasn't the Devil taken enough from you already? Are you willing to not only take back what he has stolen from you but also invade his dreams to the point of giving him nightmares? For instance, if your devil is insecurity, what if it stayed up at night dreading the fact that when you look into the mirror you would finally see that you are beautifully and wonderfully made? What if the devil keeping you from losing weight thought, "Oh no, she's on the treadmill again." What if the devil of addiction started getting agitated because you were constantly ignoring the cigarettes at the store? How would it change your life if you started affecting your devil in the same way he has affected you for so long? That's what Gideon did. He gave the enemy a taste of his own medicine.

Use your forty-day challenge to be the stuff nightmares are made of! And remember, *don't stop when you get tired.* After the initial battle, Gideon's enemy went on the run. But Gideon didn't give up.

> Then Gideon came to the Jordan and crossed over, he and
> the three hundred men who were with him, exhausted
> but still pursuing.
>
> —Judges 8:4

Wouldn't it be great if our battle with the Devil was a one-time event? We could train, prepare, and get our minds right; then we could go rushing in and claim the gold medal once and for all. If only that were the case! Your life is not a sci-fi movie. There will not be an epic battle that ends all battles.

After the battlefield you will face the minefield. This is where you will be tempted to blow yourself up again. But even when you feel exhausted from resisting the temptation, like Gideon, you must continue the pursuit. You will continue to push back the enemy as long as you stay in pursuit. And when you stay vigilant, the mission to change becomes possible. Gideon's pursuit left his enemy hanging their heads in defeat. (See Judges 8:28.)

At the end of this battle either you or your devil will hold your head high. Who will it be?

REFLECTION JOURNAL

What nightmare would you most like to give your devil?

_____

_____

_____

_____

_____

_____

_____

_____

_____

_____

_____

Real People, Real Stories

Shane's Story

Shane, a busy pastor and church planter, used his forty-day challenge to start helping his wife with the household chores. "Helping your wife clean the house may not seem like a topic you would tackle as your devil, but at my house it was an area that needed to change," he said. Shane would use his time with the devil to confront the husband he no longer wanted to be.

Shane's wife was doing all the cleaning, laundry, and cooking. This was a battle she had been fighting all by herself for the entirety of their eighteen-year marriage. To add to her already stressful workload at home, they also were the parents of a special-needs child. Shane realized that this area of their marriage had become very one-sided and that his wife was drowning under the workload.

He began day 1 by praying and asking God to help him be a better husband. As a result, God gave him a plan of action. Shane sat down with his wife and made a list of all the household chores. "I could not believe all the things she was doing that I had no idea about," he said. Then they split the list in half. For the next forty days Shane committed to partnering with his wife in the responsibility of keeping the house clean and organized.

When Shane made this commitment to his wife, she was in shock. "After eighteen years of marriage, I couldn't believe this was going to happen," she said. Shane explained that at first he wasn't all that excited about cleaning but soon got the hang of it. "It wasn't as bad as I thought," he said, "and for the first time in our marriage my wife wasn't fighting that battle by herself. I am fighting it with her!"

The results have been amazing! Shane's marriage has become stronger, and his wife no longer feels the pressure of having to do everything around the house by herself. They are happier, healthier, and closer as a result of his decision to face this devil. Several months have passed since Shane's forty-day challenge. His commitment to helping his wife is still in place.

PART VII

DON'T JUST DREAM WHILE YOU ARE ASLEEP

For a dream comes though much activity.
—ECCLESIASTES 5:3, NKJV

"May all Your enemies perish like this, O LORD! But may those who love Him rise like the sun when it rises in full strength." Then the land was at peace for forty years.
—JUDGES 5:31

A dream doesn't become reality through magic; it takes sweat, determination, and hard work.[1]
—COLIN POWELL

Day 24

DAY DREAMER

Sometimes your biggest devil is not a behavior but
a lost dream. Life becomes unfulfilling because you
have stopped chasing what your heart aches for. Today
decide to look past the odds and dream again.

Key Verse: *For a dream comes though much activity.*
—ECCLESIASTES 5:3, NKJV

FOR YOU TO experience the significant life change that
you want, you can't just dream while you are asleep. You
must do some dreaming while you are awake, "for a dream
comes through much activity" (Eccles. 5:3, NKJV).

Every dream I have seen come to fruition in my own life
followed a three-step process.

1. Identify the dream.

2. Write the dream out.

3. Carefully plan for the dream to become
   reality.

I have never accidentally accomplished anything, nor
have I achieved success by merely talking about what I
would like to do. Action always comes before activation.

Solomon taught us that our dreams aren't attained by putting words to them. You can "name it and claim it" all day,
but if you are not prepared for the activity part of making

your dreams happen, then brace yourself for a life without results. Those dreams that you have now must be activated.

Once my dreams came into focus, hard work and determination were always necessary ingredients. You can bake a pie without sugar or flour, but you will not get the desired result. All the ingredients are vital to the success of the pie. You can't leave one out.

Some of you are using this forty-day challenge to reclaim a kitchen table that has become buried under a pile of papers. For others, this journey might be the inspiration you need to go back to college. Sometimes your devil is just a lack of activity and focus. You might be using this challenge to confront a negative behavior. If that is the case, I would encourage you to carve out another forty days in the future, not to necessarily confront a behavior but to confront your laziness when it comes to chasing your dreams.

The great thing about our individuality is that we are all at different places in life. But no matter where you are in your journey, the important thing is that you continue to chase your dreams.

As a young boy I was always a day dreamer. I spent my days in elementary school staring out the window pretending to slay a dragon or make a moon landing. Well, I obviously didn't grow up to be a knight in shining armor, and I haven't had any calls lately from NASA either. At some point, I had to identify my true dreams and then make the changes required to walk in them.

As a child I always struggled with my weight, and when my wife and I got married I was carrying around about fifty extra pounds. Even though I did not yet have the concept for this book, I still applied many of the principles in these pages, and as a result I managed to lose the weight and have kept it off for over twenty years now.

On many occasions I had to, and still have to, choose a healthy meal that I honestly didn't really want over a calorie-laden meal that was more appetizing. As my friends enjoyed fried food and ice cream, I opted for grilled food and yogurt. It was not easy, to say the least! Sunday afternoon naps where replaced with Sunday afternoon workouts. A shift took place in my lifestyle. My dream was to be in reasonably good shape, and that dream was accomplished only through much activity.

I also dreamed of being a successful pastor, counselor, and author. I have seen these dreams come to pass as well, but not without work. It is important that you do more than dream. You must make the changes required to see that dream come to pass.

The only real dreams are the ones that happen while we are awake. This is an important step to changing your life. You must get gut-level honest about whatever you need to add or remove from your life. For example, if I were a smoker who wanted to stop smoking and start running marathons, I would need to remove cigarettes and add running shoes. The removal and the addition would point me in the right direction.

Once you've identified your opposition, the next step is to write it down. That is why I give you the opportunity to do that very thing in the journal section. If you don't know who your giants are, you might end up trying to slay the wrong ones.

Proverbs 29:18 tells us, "When people do not accept divine guidance, they run wild" (NLT). In the original Hebrew language the wording is a little different. Basically it says, "Where there is no vision, things get out of control." Those areas in your life that you feel are out of control, those areas that are currently consuming you, those battles you always lose are usually due to a lack of vision in that area. You have no dream.

The phrase "divine guidance" or "vision" in Proverbs 29:18 is the Hebrew word *chazon*, and it means to perceive or foresee. Usually when we are not living the life we want, it is because we have lost the ability to perceive a plan. If you knew how to change whatever is holding you back, you would have already done it, but since you don't know how, you settle in for an average life.

By now you have been given numerous tools and thoughts of encouragement in previous days. Such as:

+ Your future is waiting just beyond your willingness to confront yourself.

+ You are never going to get to where you want to be by taking shortcuts.

+ Just because you can't do it today, doesn't mean you won't be able to do it tomorrow.

+ Progress happens in your life when you decide that you certainly can.

+ Sometimes we have to get rid of the old in order
  to establish the new. You will never be successful
  by investing time in things God is trying to
  drown.

+ You will succeed when you start saying yes to the
  things that you believe you cannot do.

+ All that is separating you from your future are
  your excuses.

+ Be a nonconformist like David and rush the giant.

+ Failure is not a result of what you have done.
  Failure is a result of what you are not doing.

Now it is time to put all of that together in three different areas: planning, preparation, and people. This will be our focus for the next two days of this challenge.

You must plan, you must prepare, and you must have the right people around you if you want to live successfully. These are traits we see in Jesus. He knew not only how to plan and prepare, but He also knew how important it is to be surrounded by the right people.

Consider these questions: Do you have a plan or are you just taking life a day at a time? Are you getting prepared to step out of the mundane and into the phenomenal? Have you surrounded yourself with those who will help you get where you are going?

I learned early in life that if I want to soar with the eagles, I can't spend all of my time hanging around turkeys. I am always on the lookout for an eagle. Are you?

REFLECTION JOURNAL

Do you have a lost dream? Use your journal time today to write the dream out. Tomorrow we will focus on the plan. Today identify the dream.

_____

_____

_____

_____

_____

_____

_____

_____

_____

_____

_____

_____

_____

_____

_____

_____

_____

Day 25

A DREAM WITHOUT A PLAN IS A NIGHTMARE

Today expect to spend some time thinking about the long-range future. The Devil will no doubt try and paint a bleak picture. Decide to be an artist and paint the future you want!

Key Verse: *Go to the ant, you sluggard! Consider her ways and be wise. Which, having no guide, overseer, or ruler, provides her bread in the summer, and gathers her food in the harvest.*

—PROVERBS 6:6–8

IT'S BEEN SAID that people don't plan to fail, they just fail to plan. In my experience, however, there are a lot of people who actually do plan to fail. Sometimes we set short-range goals that can easily be achieved and then fall right back into our familiar, old ways. Without a long-range plan, especially when it comes to our opposition, we are only setting ourselves up for failure.

God is a long-range planner. If you look in Matthew chapter 1, you will find the genealogy of Jesus. It's filled with lots of hard-to-pronounce names, and to be honest, I usually skip over it when I am reading my Bible. However, if you pay close attention while reading this meticulous list of Bible characters, you will see God's long-range plan for the human race.

I have always been intrigued by the fact that God chose a harlot named Rahab to be in the lineage of Jesus. She is proof that if you change your ways and follow a different plan, your life can dramatically change. The world saw a prostitute, but God saw a grandmother for His Son.

The world will often put a label on you. Yes, like Rahab, you sometimes even deserve the label you get. But with the right plan, your label can change from prostitute to grandmother of Jesus. You may or may not be excited about being called a grandmother, but I am sure there are many other things you would like to be called—for example, healthy, on time, over it, sober, free, and committed.

God is a planner, and for you to be successful you must learn this behavior. This can be difficult, especially if your nature is to procrastinate. However, planning is essential to your success. Putting off having a plan does not change the fact that you won't move forward without one.

> Go to the ant, you sluggard! Consider her ways and be wise. Which, having no guide, overseer, or ruler, provides her bread in the summer, and gathers her food in the harvest.
>
> —Proverbs 6:6–8

Every year, when I was in elementary school, we watched an animated movie depicting the importance of planning. The scenes revolved around a bunch of hard-working ants and one lazy young grasshopper. All summer long the ants were out gathering food and getting ready for winter. The lazy grasshopper did nothing but make fun of the ants for all their efforts. As they planned and worked, he would lie in the hammock, play his guitar, and enjoy the long, lazy summer days.

As summer was nearing an end and the cool breezes of fall began to blow, the ants would warn the grasshopper of the coming winter, but he still refused to listen. It wasn't long before the temperatures fell below freezing and the snow began to fall. The ants spent their winter in the cozy den they had prepared, eating the food they had gathered and living the high life. The grasshopper froze to death.

I was a second-grader the first time I saw that movie, and the impact of the grasshopper's lack of planning is still with me to this day. I did not want to end up a grasshopper Popsicle!

All the characters in this story had the same opportunities. The difference wasn't in the opportunities; the difference was in the planning. The same is true of us. Without a plan you can only expect to fail. Without planning you can expect chaos, confusion, tiredness, feeling behind, and stress. *Time spent planning is never wasted.*

One of my favorite television shows as a child was *The A-Team*. In every episode a rough bunch of military men always seemed to get themselves into a mess, but before the end of the show they somehow managed to outsmart their opposition and save the day. The famous catchphrase from this program occurred at the end of each episode with one of the main characters saying, "I love it when a plan comes together."[1]

Without a plan, there is nothing to come together. Planning paves the way to the future you want. Your plan might need to involve a counselor, personal trainer, or other professionals. Your plan might be as simple as getting that ring around your tub cleaned up or as complex as finding a qualified therapist to help you with your childhood tragedy. Whatever your starting point, get to the place where you can say, "I love it when a plan comes together." (That was always my favorite part of the show!)

Now let's move on to a more spiritual note. I love to read the story of the Old Testament tabernacle. It was a magnificent structure, and by today's standards it would have cost millions of dollars and required the expertise of thousands of builders. It was no small task, and yet Solomon planned so far in advance the sound of a hammer was not heard at the building site.

> The house was built of stone prepared at the quarry, so that neither hammer nor axe nor any tool of iron was heard in the house while it was being built.
>
> —1 KINGS 6:7

There can be no shortage of planning: plan, plan, and then plan some more.

A dream requires a plan and a plan requires preparation. Preparation is the next step to facing the devil of lost dreams. It is necessary if you are going to win your battles. I am sure that before David ever killed a giant, he probably killed a lot of cacti! He spent a lot of time in the desert with his father's sheep, and like every teenage boy I know, he no doubt flung a few rocks. Lions, bears, and giants weren't his first victims; before he spilled blood, he spilled cactus juice!

We cannot overlook the importance of preparation. In Matthew chapter 25 we find the parable of the ten virgins. All ten had the same goal in mind, but only five were disciplined enough to be prepared.

> Then the kingdom of heaven shall be like ten virgins, who took their lamps and went out to meet the bridegroom. Five of them were wise and five were foolish. Those who were foolish took their lamps, but took no oil with them. But the wise took jars of oil with their lamps.
> —Matthew 25:1–4

The bridegroom gave specific instructions and would take only the prepared into the wedding banquet. I am trying to imagine the frustration felt by the five virgins who were uninvited to their own wedding. I am sure that when they were little girls they imagined their wedding day. They pictured themselves in bridal gowns, marrying the most handsome man in the land. Their fairy tale would soon turn to disappointment because they were not prepared. The only people in this story who found the life they were looking for were the ones who made preparation.

An unprepared person says, "Oh well, we will just figure something out when we get there." If you're not prepared, there is a good chance that, like the five foolish virgins, you won't even get there in the first place. Remember, *preparation positions you for success*. Your devil will always show up prepared. Will you?

REFLECTION JOURNAL

Now that you have written out your dream, use your journal time to write out a plan. How are you going to make your dream a reality?

_____

_____

_____

_____

_____

_____

_____

_____

_____

_____

_____

_____

_____

_____

_____

_____

_____

Day 26

HOW DID YOU GET
IN MY DREAM?

Plan on spending time today thinking about
the people in your inner circle. Are they
helping you square off against your devil? Or
are they contributing to your demise?

Key Verse: *The righteous choose their friends carefully,*
but the way of the wicked leads them astray.
—PROVERBS 12:26, NIV

COMPANIONS PREDICT YOUR future. When I was
a youth pastor, I would often tell the students, "If
you show me your friends, I will show you your future." I
have personally witnessed the catastrophic events that can
unfold just by adding one wrong person to your life. One
bad apple can spoil the entire barrel.

The people we associate with are often predictors of whether
or not we are going to have the future we want. With whom
are you choosing to spend your time? Are they contributing
to your dreams and making it easier for you to have the
future you want, or do they help you sabotage yourself?

Do not be deceived: "Bad company corrupts good morals."
—1 CORINTHIANS 15:33

I want to be an eagle and soar through life with the wind
on my wings. But I cannot do this if I spend all my time in life

with turkeys. Turkeys and eagles are very different birds. They serve two different purposes. Eagles are proud, majestic symbols of our country, and turkeys...well, turkeys are delicious!

As our key verse says, the righteous choose their friends carefully. *If companions predict the future, what do your friends tell you about yours? Before any battle can be fought, you must gather your forces.* That's what Israel's enemies always did:

> Now the Philistines gathered their armies for battle.
> —1 Samuel 17:1

I can promise you the enemy has already gathered his forces. People, circumstances, habits, familiar sins, and enemies from your past have been gathered to keep you stuck where you are. In the Christian realm this is often called spiritual warfare. If you are going to move into the excellent life you desire, you must gather your forces as well.

Consider your circle of friends because they are your forces. Do you trust them to hold the front lines? Are you willing to bet the outcome of the battle on their character? Do they help you walk the narrow path Jesus spoke of that leads to life? If not, maybe you need new forces!

> Make no friendship with an angry man, and with a furious man you will not go, lest you learn his ways and get a snare to your soul.
> —Proverbs 22:24–25

Jesus had twelve close friends. Eleven were faithful and one was a fraud. That is probably a close representation of your life. You no doubt have your Matthews and Peters, but there

is always a Judas hanging around. Before Jesus faced the opposition of the cross, He pulled the faithful closer and exposed
the fraud. You cannot skip this important step. There are
some people with whom you just can't maintain a relationship.
Embrace Aaron and eliminate Jonadab.

In Exodus 17 the children of Israel were in battle against
their enemy the Amalekites.

> Now when Moses held up his hand, Israel prevailed,
> but when he let down his hand, Amalek prevailed. But
> Moses' hands became heavy. So they took a stone, and
> put it under him, and he sat on it. And Aaron and Hur
> supported his hands, one on one side, and the other
> on the other side. And his hands were steady until the
> going down of the sun. So Joshua laid low Amalek and
> his people with the edge of the sword.
>
> —Exodus 17:11–13

When you are facing your devil, you will need Aarons.
You will need people who are willing to get in the battle
with you. They can't do the fighting for you, but their purpose is to hold you up by contributing to your life in a positive way. It might be a friend who is not afraid to tell you
the truth or a family member who stands with you as you
face the demons from your past. Whatever the case, you
need people who will help your life remain steady.

As long as Aaron and Hur were holding up Moses's arms,
everything remained steady. You also need people in your
life like Aaron, people who make you steady.

On the other hand, what about those people who help

get you into trouble, those who contribute to your weaknesses, provide for your habits, and always have a plan that leaves your life in shambles? Jonadab was such a man. When his friend Amnon came to him with a problem (the fact that Amnon was in love with his half-sister Tamar), Jonadab gave him some terrible advice.

> Jonadab instructed him, "Lie down on your bed and pretend to be ill. When your father comes to see you, say to him, 'Please allow Tamar, my sister, to come and prepare some food for me. She should make the food here, so that when I see it, I may eat it from her hand.'"
> —2 Samuel 13:5

King David's son Amnon had become so infatuated with Tamar, it made him ill. He knew the king would never permit him to marry this beautiful woman because she was such a close relative. But Amnon's friend Jonadab came up with a plan that would enable Amnon to get Tamar alone. The plan worked and Amnon ended up raping his half-sister. Later Tamar's older brother, Absalom, would kill Amnon for this action. As a result of his friendship with Jonadab, Amnon went from being a prince in Israel to being a dead rapist.

Friends like Jonadab must be eliminated from your life. The wrong people can drastically change your course.

Do you have a Jonadab in your life? Is there a friend who contributes to your weakness, helps you plot things that will only end in your destruction, and creates chaos for you? Maybe your Jonadab is an abuser, a user, or just someone who is constantly getting you off track.

You will never reach your dreams by keeping company with the Jonadabs of this life. Just like Solomon's wives would lead to his eventual demise and Sampson's relationship with Delilah would cost him his strength, the wrong people can cripple you forever.

Planning, preparing, and having the right people around you are vital. It is essential that you do not skip this crucial step. Noah did not wait until it was raining to start building the ark. David didn't pick up a slingshot for the first time as he stared down Goliath. Jesus didn't face the cross until He had first gathered the right people and exposed the wrong ones. Plan, prepare, and gather your forces.

REFLECTION JOURNAL

Be honest. Who do you need to eliminate from your inner circle? Who is your Jonadab? Now identify your Aaron. Who do you need to pull closer?

_____

_____

_____

_____

_____

_____

_____

_____

Real People, Real Stories

Belle's Story

Belle had always been thin in high school and college. However, after she got married and had children, her body began to change. Four years after the birth of her second child, she found herself still carrying the extra weight gained during pregnancy.

This is what she had to say as she approached her forty-day challenge. "I hated the way I looked on the outside because I had never been that person," she said. "I felt like a puffy marshmallow. I wanted to rid myself of the extra pounds and the destructive feelings that accompanied them. I wanted to wear clothes that looked good instead of wearing clothes that just hid my fat. I wanted to be a good example to my children so that they could see me as being confident in the way that I looked."

Belle decided that she would give God forty days and confront her weight issue. On day 1, something clicked and she felt ready to find the life she had somehow lost. She started by establishing healthy eating habits and carving out time in her already crowded schedule for exercise. She soon developed a resolve that said, "It is time for me to find the best version of myself."

Belle was able to change her life when she decided to stop making excuses for herself. She now realizes that she was the one sabotaging her desire to be thin. When I interviewed her, it had been nine months since she began her forty-day challenge, and she had reached her weight-loss goal. "When I look in the mirror, I see the real me," she said. "I see a confident woman with self-control. I can now dress like me instead of dressing like the fat version of me."

She learned that it is amazing how much you think about yourself when you don't like yourself. She is no longer living a self-absorbed life. She plans on using the forty-day concept again as she confronts other areas of her life where she desires change.

PART VIII

WANT TO TRADE?

After his suffering, he presented himself to them and gave many convincing proofs that he was alive. He appeared to them over a period of forty days and spoke about the kingdom of God.

—ACTS 1:3, NIV

Then Jacob said, "First sell me your birthright." Esau said, "Look, I am about to die; of what use is the birthright to me?"

—GENESIS 25:31–32

Day 27

YOU SHOULD BE
GLAD I AM LEAVING

God would make a terrible used car salesman.
His character is to offer us a much better deal
than we deserve. Your devil will plead his case
today. Be on guard and refuse his reasoning.
Today take the deal God is offering.

Key Verse: *He takes away the first
that He may establish the second.*
—HEBREWS 10:9

AFTER JESUS WAS resurrected, He spent the next forty days preparing His disciples for their future.

> After his suffering, he presented himself to them and gave many convincing proofs that he was alive. He appeared to them over a period of forty days and spoke about the kingdom of God.
>
> —ACTS 1:3, NIV

His future had already been decided; theirs, however, were still in question. He not only spoke to them concerning the kingdom of God but also about the things they would need to both do and add to their lives to ensure the future was successful.

In His final moments with His best friends and ministry

partners Jesus told them there would be an exchange. He would go and the Holy Spirit would come.

This was not breaking news to the disciples. Jesus had been preparing them all along.

> Nevertheless I tell you the truth: It is expedient for you that I go away. For if I do not go away, the Counselor will not come to you. But if I go, I will send Him to you.
> —John 16:7

Jesus would leave and the Holy Spirit would arrive. The new would take the place of the old. Jesus made it very clear that His departure was essential to His disciples' futures. Jesus would return to heaven and take His place at the right hand of the Father, and the Holy Spirit would replace Him on the earth and live inside the hearts of every believer.

Jesus was right—it was to the disciples' advantage that He went away. But I am sure that when He told them that, His disciples were shaking their heads in disbelief. How could life be better if their rescuer, Savior, and friend left? Little did they know, a short time later they would feel the warmth of the Holy Spirit as they gathered in the Upper Room. The fire probably felt familiar. No doubt someone shouted, "It's the master!"

From this story we learn a valuable lesson: *any time we give something to God, He will replace it with something better.*

A few years ago one of my staff members taught me a very valuable lesson on this subject. I took my family and several members of my staff out for a nice Christmas dinner. While at the restaurant our youth pastor received a phone call. His house was on fire! We immediately left and drove the fifty minutes back to where he lived. By the time we arrived, it was too late. Everything was gone. To make matters worse, it was only days before Christmas. He, his wife, and their three small children had lost everything.

The next day we went back to see if by chance anything could be salvaged. As we walked through the charred remains of what used to be the home of a happy family, I started to cry. "I am so sorry," I said.

That is when our youth pastor did something unexpected. He put his hand on my shoulder and said, "It's all right pastor. Sometimes God has to take away to establish [something new]." Like Job's friends, I was a miserable comforter that day, but I did learn that God gives beauty for ashes. It wasn't long until he and his wife found a new house. It was not only much nicer than the old house, but it was also closer to work for both him and his wife. Old appliances were soon replaced with new stainless steel ones, and once again God proved Himself faithful. The new that came was so much better than the old.

He takes away the first that He may establish the second.
—HEBREWS 10:9

As difficult as it would be for the disciples to watch Jesus ascend back to heaven, it was a necessary part of the Holy Spirit's arrival. I would have loved to have been there to hear the conversation. Peter, the outspoken leader of the group, probably said, "How can we let Him go?" God was watching and thinking, "You don't really want Him to stay. You have no idea what is coming!"

Don't be surprised if your devil tries to talk you into holding on. You will be given a list of reasons you should allow the behavior you want to change to continue unchallenged. The devil whispers, "This is what works for you. How could your life be better without me? After all, we are best friends. We need each other. We have been through so much together. Don't leave me behind. I have always been there for you." What the devil won't tell you is that if you were to let go, God would send you something much better.

The devil will fight to stay put. Jesus was no devil, but the disciples did have to be willing to make the trade. He could continue to walk with them or His Spirit could live in them. They could continue to watch Him perform miracles or they could start performing miracles themselves. They could continue walking in His footprints or they could start walking in His footsteps. The choice should have been easy, but it wasn't.

> After he said this, he was taken up before their very eyes, and a cloud hid him from their sight. They were looking intently up into the sky as he was going.
>
> —Acts 1:9–10, NIV

Instead of waving good-bye and shouting, "Don't forget to send our gift," the followers of Jesus stood with blank stares as the master flew past the clouds. Two angels would make an appearance and say, "Why do you stand here looking into the sky?"

The lesson is, at some point the disciples had to stop gazing at the clouds and start looking for the promised Holy Spirit. Soon they would leave, head for Jerusalem, and find themselves in the Upper Room. There the very thing Jesus said He would give them as an advantage would arrive.

> Suddenly a sound like a mighty rushing wind came from heaven, and it filled the whole house where they were sitting. There appeared to them tongues as of fire, being distributed and resting on each of them, 4 and they were all filled with the Holy Spirit and began to speak in other tongues, as the Spirit enabled them to speak.
>
> —ACTS 2:2–4

The mighty rushing wind of Pentecost would push the disciples—and the rest of us, I might add—forward into the future Jesus foresaw. None of it would have been possible if the first had not been taken away so that the second could be established.

Never trade the winds of Pentecost for the blowing of the devil. God is offering you a much better trade: to "provide for those who grieve in Zion—to bestow on them a crown of beauty instead of ashes, the oil of joy instead of mourning, and a garment of praise instead of a spirit of despair. They will be called oaks of righteousness, a planting of the LORD for the display of his splendor" (Isa. 61:3, NIV).

God stands ready with your "instead." Beauty, gladness, and praise would come instead of ashes, mourning, and despair. The Holy Spirit would come instead of Jesus. Good would become better, and better would become best. That's a much better deal than what the devil is offering. Take it!

REFLECTION JOURNAL

Consider your devil. Why have you held on for so long? What would you like to see God give you in place of your devil? What is your "instead of"?

_____

_____

_____

_____

_____

_____

_____

_____

_____

_____

_____

_____

_____

_____

_____

_____

Day 28

REFLECTIONS FROM THE PAST

It has been said that mirrors don't lie. This could
not be further from the truth. Today challenge
your reflection and realize that the person you
see in the mirror might just be the imposter.

Key Verse: *He made the basin of bronze with its
base of bronze from the mirrors of the women who
served at the entrance of the tent of meeting.*

—EXODUS 38:8

AFTER SPENDING FORTY days on the mountain with God,
Moses not only received the instructions for how to build
the tabernacle but also for how to furnish it. One of the key
pieces of furniture was the called the bronze basin. It stood
just outside the holy of holies in the temple courtyard. Before
the priest could enter into the presence of God, he would first
be required to stop there and wash, which is why a bronze
basin was placed at the entrance to the tent of meeting.

The basin was made of mirrors, thus casting the reflection
of the worshipper. This shows us that *before the priest could see
the glory of God, he would be forced to look at himself.*

I've tried to picture the scene in my mind. The priest
would approach the basin and plunge unclean hands into the
cool water. We can only imagine what was going through his
head as he stared at his reflection. "Is my past too much of a
disaster? After all I've done, will God accept me?" The mirror
told his story, and the mirror tells your story and mine.

Picture with me a slender middle-aged man standing in front of the mirror at the local gym. Years of proper dieting and exercise have left him in reasonably good shape. His thirty-inch waist and forty-four-inch chest are not too shabby for a forty-two-year-old! However, when this man looks in the mirror, he doesn't see a narrow waist and broad shoulders. All he can see is the twelve-year-old fat kid he used to be.

The pudgy boy looking back at him seems to have something to say. His blue eyes tell the story, a story that says, "I wish I weren't fat." His story is not unlike yours. It's a story of a past that is still trying to dictate the future. The man at the gym would rather go home and spend the next couple of hours lying in the backyard hammock or catching up after a long workday, but the fat kid in the mirror calls out and warns of a life without discipline.

The man looking in the mirror is me, and the boy on the other side of the glass is also me. I find it difficult to separate him from my thoughts. His life and mine are forever interwoven. Like two sides of the same coin, we are different yet we somehow go together. I can see the look on his face as he whispers, "Larry, are we going to be fat forever?" The reflection of my past whispers to my present.

I know that if the twelve-year-old fat kid I used to be could talk to the man I now am, he would say, "Don't waste my life. We get only one shot down here. Make the best of it." Every time I show up for a workout, the fat kid smiles and says, "I may be fat today, but one day I am going to be that man on the other side of the glass."

What if you could trade the person you currently see in

the mirror for a better version of yourself? It would still be you, only with less baggage and more confidence. How does that sound? As the late Michael Jackson sang, start with the man in the mirror; ask him to change his ways.

The man in the mirror is cheering for you! Maybe, unlike me, you've never struggled with your weight, but I am sure you've battled your self-image. The person you see in the mirror has his or her own story to tell. Maybe your image reflects depression, dysfunction, a controlling habit, divorce, or insecurity. But have you considered that the person looking back at you might not be a true representation of who you are? Obviously I am no longer a twelve-year-old fat kid.

One of the Devil's greatest tricks is to turn our mirrors into fun-house mirrors. Remember going to the local carnival and walking into the fun house? The walls were lined with mirrors. The image in the mirror was you, but it was a distorted you. Maybe your torso was stretched long or your legs were made very short. It was you, but it wasn't the real you.

The Devil wants to keep you focused on the distorted images of your past. He doesn't want you to see yourself as you really are and as God sees you. The thought of you trading your old image for a new one makes him nervous.

When I look at my reflection, I see a twelve-year-old fat kid along with many other gut-wrenching images from my past. However, I'm no longer controlled by those images. Fun house mirrors are fun to break!

When you look in the mirror, what is looking back at you? Do you see the man who has never been able to quit smoking or the woman who always allows insecurity to sabotage her relationships? Do you see the person who says, "This time it will be different," only it never is?

For you to successfully change, you must not only take responsibility for the image in the mirror, but you must also be willing to confront that image. You can escape me, and you can escape your family, but you cannot escape yourself. So if you're going to have to live with yourself for the rest of your life, you might as well roll up your sleeves and start constructing the future you want by confronting your self-image.

You can choose to be miserable with your reflection or you can chose to trade it for the real you. Make the trade! *Focus on the person you want to see in the mirror, not the person you see looking back at you.*

REFLECTION JOURNAL

Go stand in front of a mirror. What do you see? Write out your thoughts about how you see yourself. Now describe what you would like to see instead.

_____

_____

_____

_____

_____

_____

_____

_____

Day 29

WHAT WOULD YOU
TAKE FOR THAT?

Today the Devil might just offer you the easy
path. Keep in mind that there are no shortcuts
to any place worth going. The path to the future
is not always convenient. Take it anyway.

Key Verse: *Then Jacob said, "First sell me your
birthright." Esau said, "Look, I am about to
die; of what use is the birthright to me?"*
—Genesis 25:31–32

Jacob and Esau were not your typical twin brothers.
From their grooming habits to their hobbies, these two
boys could not have been more different. Esau was a man's
man. He spent his time out in the open country hunting
game and growing his beard! Jacob, on the other hand,
was content to hang around home and spend time with
his mother. Esau looked like one of those guys from *Duck
Dynasty* while Jacob would have had his own cooking show
on the Food Network. Esau could grow a beard; Jacob
could grow a garden.

> Now Jacob cooked a stew; and Esau came in from
> the field and he was famished. So Esau said to Jacob,
> "Please feed me some of that red stew, for I am famished."
> Therefore his name was called Edom.
> —Genesis 25:29–30

In a time when there was no drive-through window at McDonald's, Esau found himself in a predicament. He was famished and needed to eat but had not taken the time to prepare a meal for himself. When he arrived at home, the smell of lentil stew wafted through his nostrils. Lentils are a small, pea-like plant that was widely cultivated in the Middle East and North Africa during ancient times. When he smelled Jacob's stew, Esau probably thought, "Jacob must be home because something sure smells good." I imagine he approached and said, "Quick, give me some of that."

A quick fix usually brings a lasting mess. How many times have you taken the easy path only to realize later that it ends up taking longer than if you had done things the right way in the first place? Esau would learn this lesson. There are no shortcuts to any place worth going. What we can accomplish quickly we can lose just as fast. That is why it is so important that you finish this forty-day challenge. One day is simply not enough to assert dominance over your devil and regain control of your life. You do not want a quick fix; you want a lasting fix.

There is nothing quick about securing the future. Jacob took the time to build the fire, pick the lentils, and prepare them for dinner. Esau only showed up hungry. Both boys wanted to eat, but only one was worthy of the meal.

Then Jacob said, "First sell me your birthright."
—Genesis 25:31

The brothers were equally guilty. Both wanted to take the easy path. The meal belonged to Jacob, and the birthright belonged to Esau. A deal would be struck, and Jacob would come out on top. He left the dinner party with Esau's birthright in tow.

> Then Jacob said, "Swear to me this day." So he swore to him, and he sold his birthright to Jacob.
>
> —Genesis 25:33

The birthright didn't just give Jacob bragging rights. It established the conditions for inheritance. The oldest male child had the first rights of inheritance, meaning he would receive a far larger share of his father's estate after his father's death.

Esau traded future riches for a bowl of peas. At first glance this seems like a ridiculous trade. But upon deeper inspection, I would say this is a trade you and I have made numerous times. We trade the future for what we want right now. Consider all the times you should have suffered through the craving or the times you should have resisted the urge to do what was easy. The next time the Devil says, "Want to trade?" Remember to say, "No thanks, I don't like peas."

> Then Jacob gave Esau bread and lentil stew. Then he ate and drank, arose, and went his way. Thus Esau despised his birthright.
>
> —Genesis 25:34

It was over before he knew it. The meal he was so desperate for was now just a case of indigestion. What started off as a craving for a quick fix left Esau limping through the rest of his life. Not only did he lose the life God had arranged for him, he also resented the very thought of ever having had it. God would honor his promise to Esau's father, Isaac, and not abandon him, but Esau never fully recovered. He stands as an example of what can happen when you lose to your devil and never seek a rematch. The Apostle Paul would shed more light on this tragic story.

> See that no one is sexually immoral, or is godless like Esau, who for a single meal sold his inheritance rights as the oldest son. Afterward, as you know, when he wanted to inherit this blessing, he was rejected.
> —HEBREWS 12:16–17, NIV

Not only did Esau lose his birthright, he would also go on to lose his blessing as well. The gap between the twin boys would continue to grow. Jacob would later face his personal devils, and God would change his name to Israel. He would go on to become the father of twelve sons who would eventually become the twelve tribes of Israel. Esau's descendants weren't so lucky. A quick trade would ruin his legacy.

Esau chose convenience over commitment, and by doing so he cheated himself out of the birthright. Jacob may have arranged the deal, but Esau was the one who took it. Don't follow in his footsteps.

REFLECTION JOURNAL

In what area of your life does the Devil typically roll out the red carpet? Where does he most often tempt you to take the easy path? Will you continue to follow his alternate route?

_____

_____

_____

_____

_____

_____

_____

_____

_____

_____

_____

_____

_____

_____

_____

_____

_____

_____

Real People, Real Stories

Ginger's Story

Ginger used her forty-day challenge to confront an area of her life that had gotten completely out of hand. Her story is proof that one out-of-control behavior can affect many other aspects of our day-to-day living. This is what Ginger had to say about her forty-day challenge: "My issue might not seem big to others, but to me it was a huge problem. My quality of life was being affected. I felt tired and overwhelmed most of the time. My devil was no secret. In fact, I often joked about it. The devil I chose to face was my lack of organization."

Ginger had tried to change in the past, only to fail. She was looking for more than just good advice. Ginger was looking for biblical teaching that could help her confront her biggest enemy: herself. "I could see pieces of my personality in the biblical characters as I moved through the days," she said. "It helped me to know that I was not alone in my struggle. There were others like me."

She began by going to bed earlier the night before day 1. This way she would have more time in morning to plan her day. Day 1 started with a prayer and some preset reminders on her phone. This way she could keep her schedule organized. Ginger learned that failure is not a result of what you have done but of what you are not doing. She started making the necessary changes in her lifestyle, realizing that no one was going to do it for her.

Now that her forty-day challenge is over, Ginger said she still has room for improvement. "I am not done with my journey," she said. "I will continue to work toward my goal. Progress has been slow, but I am moving forward! I am now working to change the things that I previously ignored."

PART IX

CUT THE BULL AND MAKE THE SACRIFICE

He arranged the wood and cut the bull in pieces and laid him on the wood.

—1 KINGS 18:33

For God so loved the world that He gave His only begotten Son, that whoever believes in Him should not perish, but have eternal life.

—JOHN 3:16

Day 30

CUT THE BULL

The devil wants you to make excuses for yourself. That way you don't feel responsible when you lose the fight. Don't cop out! With knife in hand, challenge those excuses.

Key Verse: *He arranged the wood and cut the bull in pieces and laid him on the wood.*

—1 KINGS 18:33

BEFORE THE PROPHET Elijah was ready to face the obstacles standing in the way of his future, he would first need to face himself and "cut the bull"!

Elijah was part of an epic showdown with the prophets of Baal to prove whose god was the true and living God. Here he explains the rules:

> "Therefore, let them give us two bulls, and let them choose one bull for themselves and cut it in pieces and lay it on some wood, but do not light a fire under it, and I will prepare the other bull, lay it on some wood, and not light a fire underneath it. And you call on the name of your gods, and I will call on the name of the LORD, and the God that answers by fire, let Him be God." And all the people answered and said, "It is well spoken."
>
> —1 KINGS 18:23–24

After both sides agreed on the terms, Elijah upped the ante for the God of Abraham, Isaac, and Jacob.

He arranged the wood, *cut the bull* into pieces and laid it on the wood. Then he said to them, "Fill four large jars with water and pour it on the offering and on the wood."

"Do it again," he said, and they did it again.

"Do it a third time," he ordered, and they did it the third time. The water ran down around the altar and even filled the trench.

At the time of sacrifice, the prophet Elijah stepped forward and prayed.

—1 KINGS 18:33–36, NIV, EMPHASIS ADDED

I am sure you know the rest of the story. God sent the fire and burned up the sacrifice.

This must have looked like a scene from a Hollywood movie. Picture an entire nation gathered around a mountain to watch a showdown between one man of God and 950 men who claimed to know a different god. This epic battle would forever change Elijah's life.

The rules were simple: both Elijah and the prophets of Baal would prepare a sacrifice and the god who answered by fire would be recognized as the true God. The prophets of Baal were first to try to entice their god to answer. They jumped, danced, shouted, and everything else we do to whip up a good church service. But no one answered, no one cared, and no one paid any attention.

Elijah is my kind of guy, because he even began to taunt his opposition. He said, "Maybe your god is taking a nap, or perhaps he is on a vacation." (See 1 Kings 18:27.)

I can hear the sarcasm in his voice. After hours of begging Baal to answer, the false prophets finally gave up. Then Elijah stepped up and did two very interesting things before he got the result he was seeking. *He cut the bull and made the sacrifice!*

I know, I know, it was an actual animal, and the sacrifice was an offering made to God. However, I see much more in this story. If you are going to get the result you want, you must cut the bull and make the sacrifice, just as Elijah did.

Just cut the bull already! Will you always make excuses for why you can't, why it's too hard, and why you're different from the rest of us?

Sacrifice is defined as forfeiting one thing for another thing considered to be of greater value. It's letting something of lesser value go so you can add something of greater value to your life. For example, if you let go of smoking, you can add many years of healthy living. While nicotine might feed your addiction, it is of far less value than your health.

Elijah's message to the nation of Israel was simple, "Let Baal go and go after God." In other words, trade the lesser for the greater and the counterfeit for the real. For you, that would mean exchanging the familiar behaviors for a better life.

Consider again the words of Elijah.

> Elijah came to all the people and said, "How long will you stay between two opinions?"
>
> —1 KINGS 18:21

That verse is sobering because it reflects the way our lives look so much of the time. We waver and waffle. One day we feel like we have it all together, and the next day we feel like we are coming apart. Apparently the nation of Israel had not completely sold out to Baal. They still seemed conflicted.

They knew what to do but didn't always do it. Does that sound familiar?

Baal represented everything that stood in their way. This false god's negative influence was far-reaching, which was why they had to let him go.

Will you let those negative things from your past go? Will you sacrifice present comfort? Will you take those things you identified early in this book as problem areas and lay them on the altar of sacrifice? In order to get to a life of greater value, you must first let those things of lesser value go. You must make the sacrifice!

I am sure the bull in this story was a fine animal, the kind that would win a blue ribbon at the county fair. Nevertheless, it had to be cut and sacrificed to God.

After this showdown Elijah would go on to face his greatest opposition, the evil King Ahab and Queen Jezebel. Even though he felt like dying, he did not, and I believe it was because he had learned that when life gets tough, he had to cut the bull!

Cutting the bull was hard work. Elijah didn't run down to the local market and get nicely packaged bull pieces. No, it was a bloody, sweaty, and tedious task.

When I was a child, my dad spent many years as a local butcher. On more than one occasion, I stood and watched him "cut the bull." There was nothing glorious about the scene. It was brutal and difficult. However, it always brought a reward. I just love T-bones!

For you to be successful in changing your life, pick up the figurative knife, roll up your sleeves, and make the slice.

It will be a bloody, messy job, and the bull is going to resist!
Cut anyway!

REFLECTION JOURNAL

*Do you need to cut the bull? What excuses have you always
relied upon in the past to take you out of the fight?*

_____

_____

_____

_____

_____

_____

_____

_____

_____

_____

_____

_____

_____

_____

_____

Day 31

YOU CAN'T HANDLE
THE TRUTH

What if everything you have been telling yourself about
your devil is a lie? How would that change your life?
Today be willing to "cut the bull" when it comes to your
behavior by confronting what you perceive to be true.

Key Verse: *You shall know the truth,*
and the truth shall set you free.

—JOHN 8:32

ONE OF THE hardest things to do is tell ourselves the
truth. We often skirt around it, twist it, and even
avoid it. Pretending is always easier because it removes us
from personal responsibility. As you learn to "cut the bull,"
you will have to start with yourself and what you believe
about your devils. Are you telling yourself the truth? Your
attitude will determine the outcome. The objective is for
you to do more than just change for forty days. The objective is for you to change for the remainder of your days.
This will require more than a Band-Aid or a temporary
remedy. You will need surgery. Every lie and false notion
you have repeated to yourself over the years must be carefully cut away.

Permanent change is rooted in truth. First, begin by asking
yourself, "Can I handle the truth?" Remember the movie *A
Few Good Men*? In this film a court martial lawyer exposes

a highly decorated colonel for his false testimony surrounding the death of marine. From this movie we get the famous line, "You can't handle the truth!"[1] Sadly this is all too true for many of us. Since we can't handle the truth, we devise plans to ignore it. The problem with ignoring any reality is it doesn't change the truth. If lasting change is what you are after, it always starts with the truth.

One of the titles given to the Devil is the "father of lies" (John 8:44). This is not an accident. To be successful in changing, you must see your devils in the same manner. The Devil is simply not capable of telling the truth. Everything he says must always be questioned. From the Garden of Eden to the present, the Devil has always used deception as his chief tactic.

Behind every lie there is a plan for your demise. If the Devil can ever get you to question the truth, you are in trouble. That is why it is imperative that you cut the bull when it comes to your daily dialogue with yourself.

> Finally, brothers, whatever things are true, whatever things are honest, whatever things are just, whatever things are pure, whatever things are lovely, whatever things are of good report, if there is any virtue, and if there is any praise, think on these things.
>
> —PHILIPPIANS 4:8

Pay close attention to the list of adjectives Paul uses in his effort to direct our thought lives. First comes truth—and is it any wonder? Truth is vital to our success. Our problem is often that we spend too much time thinking about things that are rooted in lies rather than things that are rooted in truth. It is impossible to live a positive life when you have negative thinking.

Truth makes life excellent and praiseworthy. The Bible is clear when it comes to our need for truth. We are told to walk in it, seek after it, know it, desire it, be established in it, rightly divide it, and learn to love it. Nowhere in that list in Philippians 4:8 are the words "ignore it." Ignoring the truth is the same as embracing the lie.

Scripture is full of those who both rejected and ignored the truth. The consequences were always fatal.

If the truth sets us free as John 8:32 says, then obviously we stay in bondage every time we refuse to accept it—in bondage to our past, circumstances, habits, and hang-ups. This verse is talking about Jesus, but it also applies directly to our lives. Truth is freedom—real freedom.

Are you ready to cut the bull when it comes to what you tell yourself about yourself? Will you allow the Holy Spirit to reveal to you the real culprit behind every battle with the devil you have lost in the past? Can you handle the truth?

> Stand firm then, with the belt of truth buckled around your waist.
> —Ephesians 6:14, niv

Without a belt you can be caught with your pants down. This is not a mistake you can afford to make with the Devil. He is relentless and will no doubt capitalize on any vulnerability in your life. The belt of truth holds the rest of the armor together. Simply put, truth keeps us from falling apart. Buckle your belt. You can't fight with your pants down.

REFLECTION JOURNAL

Identify the areas where you are not being completely honest with yourself. How will you place the belt of truth around those areas?

_____

_____

_____

_____

_____

_____

_____

_____

_____

_____

_____

_____

_____

_____

_____

Day 32

HOW I CUT THE BULL: A MARATHON JOURNEY

Sometimes a setback can become a setup.
What if you found a way around your biggest
obstacles? Today, picture the Devil in wide-
eyed disbelief that you are actually doing it!

Key Verse: *But those who wait upon the LORD
shall renew their strength; they shall mount up
with wings as eagles, they shall run and not be
weary, and they shall walk and not faint.*

—ISAIAH **40:31**

RECENTLY I EXPERIENCED firsthand what it's like to cut
the bull and make the sacrifice. This book is about so
much more than just helping you get past destructive habits
and negative behaviors. It is also very much about helping
you achieve your best and reach your goals.

One of my fitness goals was to run a marathon before
the age of forty. I know, I know, ironic, right? For this to
happen, I knew it would require tremendous sacrifice. Six
months before my fortieth birthday, I rolled up my sleeves,
picked up the knife, and cut the bull. Oh, I also bought
some running shoes. It was time to train for a marathon!

Until that point I had never run more than four miles,
and even then I had to stop from time to time to catch

my breath. So the 26.2-miles would require a four-month training commitment.

Any time you have a dream bigger than you, you must have a determination bigger than your doubts. If I had begun my journey thinking, "I'll give it a shot and see how hard it is," I would have quit on the first day. No, I decided I would not just train to finish, I would train to win. If I were to accomplish this task, a sacrifice would have to be made. Little did I know that sacrifice would be me!

My journey began January 7, 2013, as two friends and I began our training. The fat kid in the mirror was about to become a marathon runner. We began by consulting with a local group of runners and found a sixteen-week marathon-training program. We then went online to select the marathon we would be competing in. As luck would have it, the Saint Jude Rock and Roll marathon in Nashville, Tennessee, was scheduled to take place just when we would be completing our training. Before we even started training, we registered to run, thinking it would be fun to travel from Missouri to Nashville in the spring.

If you are going to succeed in accomplishing your goals, you must look ahead to the results you seek. Before we ran the first step, we planned to succeed. We did not give ourselves the option of quitting or turning back. Our goal had been identified, and we determined to make the necessary sacrifice. This was crucial to our success. Instead of focusing on the difficulty of the training, we focused on the finish line.

I remember the first day of training. It was a cold January day. The temperature was in the twenties and the wind was blowing hard. I met my friends at a local park that had a running track, and we began the sixteen-week march to our goal. When we finished that first three-mile run, I think we all understood why less than 1 percent of people on the planet run marathons.

The thought of running another twenty-three miles seemed ridiculous and far beyond our capabilities, but we would continue to run anyway.

Winters in Missouri are often unpredictable. One day it can be in the seventies with sunshine, and the next day it can be in the thirties with freezing rain. I'm not sure what we were thinking when we decided to train in this kind weather, but we knew there was no turning back.

All dreams can come true if you have the courage to pursue them. As the weeks went by, we ran. We ran while others took naps. We ran when the fish were biting. We ran on the days when our clothes would freeze because of the rain and cold temperatures. We ran in the snow. We ran when we were sick. We ran when others said, "You have to be crazy to run on a day like today!" Like Forrest Gump, we ran just for the sake of running! No matter what the obstacle, we kept moving toward our goal.

At about week 10, I injured my foot. I had a condition known as plantar fasciitis due to the excessive pounding on my feet during long runs. It literally felt like someone was sticking a hot poker in my heel every time I put weight on it. It would have been easy for me to quit. I could barely walk, let alone run. I felt like my injury was trying to keep me from reaching my goal. My body was staging a revolt. This was a setback I was not expecting. Getting injured during training had never crossed my mind.

When you're straining to reach your goal, there will always be setbacks. After I injured my foot, I had a choice to make: Do I use the legitimate excuse of being injured to abandon my dream or do I find a way around the mountain in front of me?

I chose to find a way around the mountain. I found a man in my area who is a renowned extreme marathon runner. I told him of my injury, and he immediately knew what to do. He told me to take a tennis ball and use it to massage the injured area for three days. It worked! After three days there was no more pain!

Don't let the setback become a setup. Sometimes God is using what looks like setbacks to set us up for what He desires for us. But if wallow in self-pity or get disillusioned and refuse to move forward, setbacks can set us up for failure. The key to overcoming a setback is to simply find another way to keep moving forward. My injury sidelined me for less than a week, only because I took the initiative.

Don't let your setbacks derail you from pursuing your destiny. If you do, you'll be playing right into the Devil's hands. Remember, you can do all things through Christ who gives you strength.

REFLECTION JOURNAL

Do you have a personal goal, perhaps something on your bucket list? What has kept you from beginning your journey to making it a reality?

_____

_____

_____

_____

_____

_____

_____

_____

_____

_____

_____

_____

_____

_____

_____

_____

_____

_____

Day 33

HITTING THE WALL

The most difficult mile in a marathon is mile twenty. This is where you hit the wall. You may feel like you are at your mile twenty today, but keep running. If the wall hits you, hit back!

Key Verse: *For by You I can run through a troop, and by my God I can leap a wall.*
—PSALM 18:29

My TRAINING FOR my first marathon intensified during the last six weeks. My buddies and I were running close to fifty miles a week and pushing our bodies to their absolute limits. There was lots of cramping, throwing up, and feeling completely exhausted. The only thing worse than the run itself was the day after—every joint in my body would ache. But I couldn't give up. This almost forty-year-old wasn't just training to finish; I was training to win.

Do you not know that all those who run in a race run, but one receives the prize? So run, that you may obtain it.
—1 CORINTHIANS 9:24

I was running to win the prize, but I remember one eighteen-mile run that almost ended my quest. At about mile sixteen I literally could not make my legs work. They simply decided not to run anymore. In the running world this is called hitting the wall. But I didn't just hit a wall; I hit the entire house!

More accurately I felt like the house had hit me. I sat down on the edge of the road and started to call my wife to come and pick me up. I felt defeated. The race was three weeks away, and I was not even close to running over twenty miles at that point—or so I thought.

Before I dialed my wife's number, I thought to myself, "Larry, you're only two miles from home, and you're going to do this even if you have to crawl!" Five minutes went by, and I stood to my feet. I started walking and thought, "Hey, this isn't so bad!" It wasn't long before I had once again found my stride, and the next thing I knew I was standing on my front porch. Less than thirty minutes earlier I was about to call it quits, but now I had finished my run. The difference between success and failure was less than thirty minutes. *The biggest obstacle between you and your goals is what you do when you hit the wall.*

The wall is anything that stands in your way. For me, it was legs that no longer wanted to run. For you, it might be a financial loss. For a friend of mine in politics, it was a lost election. But he said, "This is just a setback. I will be back!" The wall is the proverbial stopping place just short of your goal. When your wall hits you, hit back!

The next week I was scheduled to run twenty miles on a Saturday morning. My running partners could not run with me that day, so I was on my own. The first ten miles were a breeze, but as I started getting closer to that sixteen-mile mark, my mind went back to the previous week. I thought to myself, "Oh boy, my legs are going to give out again. I just know it."

However, when I hit the sixteen-mile mark this time, there was no wall! I ran right through it! Before I knew it I was at mile eighteen. Then I hit mile nineteen, and I was still running. A smile came to my lips as I crossed the twenty-mile mark, and to my amazement I felt like I could keep going. The wall had hit me hard the previous week, but not this week. This week, I had hit back. *For by Him I can run through a troop, and by my God I can leap a wall.*

It was now week 15, and for the first time I felt like my goal of completing a marathon was within my grasp. I had cut the bull, made the sacrifice, and not wavered. It was time to race!

The marathon was on April 27, and boy, were we in for a shock. Typically the weather in Tennessee that time of year is perfect for running, but this day was anything but typical. We awoke to pouring rain and temperatures in the lower forties. The forecast was grim.

Over the next few hours several inches of rain were expected to fall and believe me, it fell! We stood on Broadway Street in downtown Nashville with thirty thousand other runners in blinding rains, frigid temperatures, and strong winds. The starting gun went off, and we headed into what seemed like a hurricane. The streets were flooding, and at times we were running in water that came almost to our knees. An already difficult day became even more difficult!

It wasn't hard to identify those who had not made the sacrifice in the previous weeks. The untrained were dropping like flies! I was running beside a group who had spent the winter training indoors, and they were ill-prepared to race on a day like this. They had opted for the comfort of a heated gym rather than the discomfort of a frozen highway, and it showed. Before long, they slowly began to give up one by one. But not me! I was trained, toned, and ready to run in any weather conditions, because unlike so many others I had prepared. My weight had gone from 176 pounds to 154 pounds, and my body fat had fallen from 18 percent to 14.7 percent.

I had done everything I could possibly do to position myself to succeed. *Sacrifice had prepared me for the finish line.*

It wasn't easy, and there were definitely times along the way when I wanted to give up. There were times when my body was cramping, times when those running alongside me were quitting, and times when it seemed I couldn't run another step. I was only able to finish because I had previously spent the time confronting my flesh and pushing myself to do my very best.

My goal was to finish in less than five hours. I missed my goal by a mere nine minutes! Needless to say, I did not win first place. However, my five hour and nine minute finish wasn't what I was thinking about when they put the medal around my neck. I was thinking, "The fat kid in the mirror is now a marathon runner!"

It was no accident that my marathon journey took place while I was writing this book. I learned firsthand what kind of discipline and sacrifice are necessary to achieve your best. Not cutting the bull is not an option if you want to be a champion.

You will never run a marathon if you're unwilling to confront your weakness and sacrifice your comfort. In the same

way you will never realize your dreams and accomplish your
goals if you won't confront the person you've always been.

Before my training began, I was in good shape, but now
I'm in great shape. Good wasn't enough to get me across
the finish line. I needed something more. I needed to cut
the bull, make the necessary sacrifices, and prepare myself
for the road ahead.

Champions are self-made. I hope you'll use the principles in this book to find the champion inside you!

REFLECTION JOURNAL

*Think about the obstacles that strike back at you, the points where
you sense something putting its hand in your face and saying, "No
further." The next time you hit the wall, how will you hit back?*

_____

_____

_____

_____

_____

_____

_____

_____

_____

_____

_____

PART X

CHANGE IS POSSIBLE WHEN YOU HAVE HAD ENOUGH

He went a day's journey into the wilderness and came and sat down under a juniper tree and asked that he might die, saying, "It is enough! Now, O LORD, take my life, for I am not better than my fathers."

—1 KINGS 19:4

If you don't change direction, you may end up where you are heading.[1]

—LAO TZU

We cannot achieve our wildest dreams by remaining who we are.[2]

—JOHN C. MAXWELL

Day 34

I HAVE HAD ENOUGH

At some point you just get sick and tired of being
sick and tired. Plan to experience both today.
Change usually occurs when it is the only option.

Key Verse: *He came to a broom bush, sat down under it
and prayed that he might die. "I have had enough, LORD,"
he said. "Take my life; I am no better than my ancestors."*
—1 KINGS 19:4, NIV

ONE OF THE most difficult things to do in life is to
change, and yet it is absolutely essential if you are
going to have the future you truly want. The person you
want to be is not going to just show up one day at your
doorstep and assume your identity. The person you want to
be is waiting for you to show up.

To change is to become different or make somebody or
something different; it means to exchange, substitute, or
replace something. When I think of change, my mind always
goes to the caterpillar. I have always felt sorry for our fuzzy
little friend because no one hears him screaming from inside
the cocoon. We often bask in the beauty of butterflies, but
we forget about the journey it took to get there. The cocoon
is a place of solitude, pain, and change. But it is also the place
where the fuzzy little worm becomes a monarch!

Inside of you is the insatiable desire to be something, do
something, or change something. Those feeling must not

be ignored. The reason you want these things so badly is because they are part of who God created you to be. They are the real you. When you're not experiencing what your heart aches for, life becomes frustrating.

Failure is not a result of what you have done. Failure is a result of what you are not doing. If you are serious about changing your life, then you must be prepared to change yourself. One of my favorite quotes comes from John C. Maxwell, "We cannot achieve our wildest dreams by remaining who we are." This quote has hung on the wall in my office for years, and I read it many times every day. This is true for all of us. It doesn't matter if you are a middle-age mom who wants to run a marathon or a man who would like to stop drinking a gallon of coffee every day. The only way forward is to change.

Change is possible when you have had enough!

In order for you to experience the change necessary to move into the future you desire, you must do more than talk about, want it, or even pray about. You must, like Elijah, come to the place of "I have had enough!"

Elijah is one of my favorite Old Testament characters because he wasn't afraid to take a stand for what he believed, even when it wasn't popular. And yet even Elijah had times of great depression. Consider this account.

Now Ahab told Jezebel everything Elijah had done and how he had killed all the prophets with the sword. So Jezebel sent a messenger to Elijah to say, "May the gods deal with me, be it ever so severely, if by this time tomorrow I do not make your life like that of one of them."

Elijah was afraid and ran for his life. When he came to Beersheba in Judah, he left his servant there, while he himself went a day's journey into the wilderness. He came to a broom bush [or tree], sat down under it and prayed that he might die. "I have had enough, LORD," he said. "Take my life; I am no better than my ancestors." Then he lay down under the bush and fell asleep.

All at once an angel touched him and said, "Get up and eat." He looked around, and there by his head was some bread baked over hot coals, and a jar of water. He ate and drank and then lay down again.

The angel of the LORD came back a second time and touched him and said, "Get up and eat, for the journey is too much for you." So he got up and ate and drank. Strengthened by that food, he traveled forty days and forty nights until he reached Horeb, the mountain of God. There he went into a cave and spent the night.

And the word of the LORD came to him: "What are you doing here, Elijah?"

—1 KINGS 19:1–9, NIV

This story has always intrigued me because Elijah had experienced one of his greatest victories just prior to this encounter with Jezebel. You remember the story of Mount Carmel, where God sent fire from heaven and proved Himself to be the only true God. Well, now none of that seemed to matter. Elijah had many areas of victory under his belt, but there was still that one particular place where the enemy always seemed to be able to get him.

Do you have an area were the enemy always seems to

have the upper hand? That go-to place where your devil is trying to keep you from being the person you want to be? Elijah had this same problem. He had a broom tree. This is the place where you sit down and say, "I can't go on anymore." It's where you can't see any way to have a good future. At the broom tree hope gets lost.

I can picture Elijah slumped over, arms crossed, and thinking to himself, "This is it. Nobody cares, nobody is on my side, and nobody understands how I feel. I'm done!" Do you have a broom tree? Do you feel as if you can't keep going? Are you done? Elijah was a powerful prophet and yet completely human. Spiritual maturity does not impress the devil.

Before Elijah could go on a forty-day journey that would change his life, he had to get to the place of "I have had enough!" Before you can experience lasting change, you too must get to that place, the place that says, "I don't want to live this way another day; I have had enough! I don't want to continue down this road of unhealthy living; I've had enough! I don't want to keep hanging on to resentment and anger; I've had enough! I refuse to continue to allow my past to poison my future; enough already!"

Right now think about all the things you want to change, the things keeping you from the dreams you want to realize and the goals you want to achieve. Say to each one of them, "I have had enough!" In fact, you might need to say that every day through the remainder of your forty-day challenge.

After Elijah had had enough, he was ready to begin his forty-day journey to the mountain of God. When you have had enough, then you'll be ready to move forward into what

God has for you as well. It won't be easy, and your familiar enemies will fight you every step of the way, just as Elijah's familiar enemies fought against him.

But after Elijah made it through his forty-day journey, we never again find him begging God to die. Suddenly he found life worth living. The same hope and optimism about the future can well up in you if you'll decide, "Enough is enough!"

REFLECTION JOURNAL

Think about the areas where you have had enough. What are you going to do about them? Use your journaling time today to list them. Write out beside each one, "I have had enough."

_____

_____

_____

_____

_____

_____

_____

_____

_____

_____

_____

_____

Day 35

WHO IS YOUR ELISHA?

One of the greatest motivators when seeking
change are those we know we need to
change for. Today, allow God to speak to you
concerning those who are counting on you.

Key Verse: *So he [Elijah] departed from there and
found Elisha the son of Shaphat, who was plowing
with twelve yoke of oxen before him and he with the
twelfth, and Elijah passed by him and threw his cloak
on him. He left the oxen and ran after Elijah.*

—1 KINGS 19:19–20

WHEN ELIJAH SAT down under the broom tree and
said, "I have had enough," he had no idea that his
willingness to either face his devil or be destroyed by his
devil would directly impact the life and ministry of a man
named Elisha. After Elijah got up and traveled forty days
and forty nights to the mountain of God, he received these
instructions: "Anoint Elisha son of Shaphat from Abel
Meholah to succeed you as prophet" (1 Kings 19:16, NIV).

At the broom tree Elijah had no knowledge of Elisha
or the ministry that would result from his encounter with
him. When Elijah sat down under that tree, his only focus
was what he perceived to be an unwinnable battle. He was
not looking toward the future, nor was he focusing on
those who were counting on him to face his devil. All he

saw was Jezebel. *Consider the people in your world who are counting on you, both the known and the unknown.*

Obviously the "known" are easy to spot. Children, spouses, family members, and friends are greatly impacted when we, like Elijah, decide the battle cannot be won. Our decision to either face our devils or continue to run from them will greatly impact their futures.

Elijah failed to see how his behavior would affect the people in his world. Don't do the same. Consider the known people in your life who need you to rise up, face the devil, and help pave the road to a smooth future. Facing your devil is not just for your benefit; it is also for theirs as well.

The "unknown" people are not as easy to spot. As far as we know, at this point in Elijah's life, he and Elisha had never crossed paths. While it is probable that Elisha had heard of Elijah, they likely met for the first time when Elijah set out to do what God instructed.

> So he departed from there and found Elisha the son of Shaphat, who was plowing with twelve yoke of oxen before him and he with the twelfth, and Elijah passed by him and threw his cloak on him. He left the oxen and ran after Elijah and said, "Please let me kiss my father and mother, and then I will follow you." And he said to him, "Go back, for what have I done to you?"
>
> —1 KINGS 19:19–20

This farmer-turned-prophet had no idea that his future hinged on Elijah's willingness to face his past. Your future is filled with people waiting to feel your cloak as you cast your influence upon them. They are your Elishas.

Early in this book I referenced a period of temptation in my own life. My devil was not only trying to get me to throw away what had been, he was also trying to get me to throw away what was to come. At the time I had no idea I would write this book or that the people who would one day read it would become my Elishas.

You are the unknown person I was unaware of during my time in the desert. I fought for you. Will you fight for others?

REFLECTION JOURNAL

Who are the known Elishas in your life? What can you do to contribute to their futures?

_____

_____

_____

_____

_____

_____

_____

_____

_____

_____

PART XI

MUMMY-MAKING IS SERIOUS BUSINESS

Then Joseph fell on his father's face and wept over him and kissed him. Joseph commanded his servants the physicians to embalm his father. So the physicians embalmed Israel. Forty days were required for him, for such is the time required for those who are embalmed. Then the Egyptians mourned for him seventy days.

—GENESIS 50:1–3

Truly, truly I say to you, unless a grain of wheat falls into the ground and dies, it remains alone. But if it dies, it bears much fruit.

—JOHN 12:24

Day 36

SOMEBODY HAS TO
MAKE THE MUMMY

Now that you are nearing the end of this challenge,
no doubt parts of your flesh have been crucified
with Christ and are ready for burial. Use today
to focus on those things that are still very much
alive and creating a foul odor in your life.

Key Verse: *So the physicians embalmed Israel.
Forty days were required for him, for such is the
time required for those who are embalmed. Then
the Egyptians mourned for him seventy days.*

—GENESIS 50:2–3

W HEN I WAS a kid, I never liked going to the funeral
home. It always seemed creepy to me, and even now
that I am an adult I'm not crazy about the thought of
others one day staring at my dead body! Displaying what
is left behind just seems like an odd way to celebrate someone's life. Maybe it's just me, but I think it's a little weird.

All cultures throughout time have made provisions for
their bodies after death. In Scripture we read how Jacob's
body was preserved after he passed away.

Joseph commanded his servants the physicians to embalm
his father. So the physicians embalmed Israel. Forty days
were required for him, for such is the time required for

those who are embalmed. Then the Egyptians mourned
for him seventy days.
—GENESIS 50:1–3

The Egyptians were meticulous when it came to their
practice of embalming. It was a tedious process that involved
removing organs and adding various spices and oils. The
body was then wrapped in fresh linen and usually placed in
a man-made tomb or cave. The old was dealt with carefully.

Once again in this Old Testament story we find the number
forty. It is no accident that forty is the number of days required
for embalming. For forty days the old had to be confronted
and carefully handled. That's what you've been doing on this
journey. And now with each passing day, the old remains of
your past are coming closer to being ready for burial.

Before Jacob died he gave very clear instructions about
how he wanted to be buried.

> Then he charged them and said to them, "I am about to
> be gathered to my people. Bury me with my fathers in
> the cave that is in the field of Ephron the Hittite.
—GENESIS 49:29

The old had to be disposed of because the old can really
stink things up if you don't bury it properly. When Jesus
raised Lazarus from the dead, Lazarus had been in the
grave for only four days and his sister said, "Lord, surely he
stinks by now." (See John 11:39.)

Since you're reading this book, there's a good chance that
some part of your life stinks. It is undoubtedly connected to
your old way of life, and you've probably already identified

it as your devil. So, as Jacob did, will you declare: "Bury me! Bury my eating disorder! Bury my bad habits! Bury my destructive behaviors! Bury the person I've become!"?

Joseph threw himself on his father, wept, and kissed him. However, he realized that he had to leave the old to the embalmers. For forty days he had to hand over his father's body to follow his wishes and then bury him with his fathers.

Somebody had to make the mummy. In Jacob's story it was the professionals. In your story, it's you. The process isn't really all that different. To be a professional mummy-maker you really only need to remove the things you no longer need and replace them with some spice. When I was a teenager, my first real bottle of cologne was a bottle of Old Spice I was given one year for Christmas. I am not sure if it helped me attract girls, but I am sure that it alerted them to my presence. When you use half the bottle at once, others can smell you long before they can see you!

Your life also has a fragrance, and you can choose to smell dead or you can choose to submit to forty days of embalming and add some spice to your life so it will be a sweet-smelling fragrance to God (2 Cor. 2:15). That is what this challenge is all about.

After the forty days of embalming took place, the last step was to wrap the body in fresh, clean linen. I know what you're thinking. In the mummy movies the monster is always dingy and dirty, and the wraps look pretty old. But this is not Hollywood and the reality is, once the old has been carefully dealt with, it gets clothed in the new. The new is fresh, clean, and so much better!

> Since, then, we do not have the excuse of ignorance,
> everything—and I do mean everything connected with
> that old way of life has to go. It's rotten through and
> through. Get rid of it! And then take on an entirely new
> way of life—a God-fashioned life, a life renewed from
> the inside and working itself into your conduct as God
> accurately reproduces his character in you.
>
> —EPHESIANS 4:22–24, THE MESSAGE

In these verses, the Apostle Paul makes it very clear: before you can take on an entirely new way of life, everything connected to the old way of life has to go. He then tells us why—"It's rotten through and through."

The things connecting you to the old are keeping you trapped in your behavior. I have heard it said, "Don't burn bridges; you might need to cross them again someday." But when it comes to the bridges connecting you to the person you no longer want to be, you must break the connection.

After the embalming process, the old has to be buried. This step cannot be skipped. After your forty-day journey, there will be many occasions in which the rotten will try to return. Joseph was required to leave his father with the embalmers for a "full" forty days; then his body was ready to be buried, not to be put on display. What if you looked at the remainder of this challenge as a requirement? No excuses, no slipping back into old familiar patterns, and no days off—just you and Pharaoh's morticians getting the dead things in your life ready for burial.

Part of the reason we sometimes go our entire lives without ever confronting our devils and making the changes we want to make is because we are not required to do so. There is no time "required for embalming." There is no one to force us to change, so we just stay the same. The same is easier and familiar, but it is also the bridge connecting you to the person you no longer want to be. There are only a few things in life that are required, such as nourishment, water, and sleep—and death and taxes! Everything else is a choice.

What if you were required to face your devil and spend some time on the embalmer's table properly dealing with the dead things in your life? No one can force you to confront yourself. If the mummy gets made, you will have to do the wrapping.

REFLECTION JOURNAL

Rotten behavior often results in a stinky life. Consider the foul odors in your life. Where are they coming from? How will you add some spice?

_____

_____

_____

_____

_____

_____

_____

_____

Day 37

I CAN'T BELIEVE
YOU ARE DEAD

Today you might experience what we would call
withdrawal. You are nearing the finish line, and
the Devil will likely make a run at you.

Key Verse: *When Jacob finished instructing
his sons, he drew his feet into the bed, breathed
his last, and was gathered to his people.*

—GENESIS **49:33**

I HAVE NEVER BEEN a fan of scary movies, but I have seen a few. The plot is always the same. A terrified group of unsuspecting young people encounter a monster of some kind. They eventually figure out a way to kill it—or so they think. Once it's dead, they celebrate, but the celebration is usually short-lived because the monster always finds a way to return. Make sure this doesn't happen to you. Remember, old things have passed away and the new has come (2 Cor. 5:17).

After Jesus was crucified, He returned from the dead. Your devil will always try to mimic the Savior, but it will never be anything more than a cheap counterfeit. Your devil will also try to come back, but you must take every precaution to ensure that does not happen. That means you must be prepared for the grief.

When Jacob died, after the initial forty days of embalming, thirty days were set aside for grieving, bringing the total number of days to seventy (Gen. 50:3). Any time we experience a loss, we can always expect some grief, and no doubt Joseph and the rest of his family grieved as they missed their father. However, the grieving period eventually came to an end.

> When the days of his mourning were past…
> —GENESIS 50:4

After you have submitted to the embalming process and have spent forty days squaring off with your devil, expect some grief. The next thirty days will be crucial to your success. Start preparing yourself for them right now. You will no doubt experience some grieving, and the loss of the familiar will be fresh on your mind. Even when your devil is destructive, it is still very much a part of you. You may even feel as if you have lost a close relative.

The good news is, there will come a time when the days of mourning will pass. It probably won't be as soon as you would like it to be, but eventually you will stop missing the behavior you were seeking to change.

For example, if you have spent the last twenty years struggling with an eating disorder and you decide to use your forty-day challenge to conquer something as serious as bulimia, it won't be easy once the forty-day "embalming process" is complete. It will require you to completely change how you approach each meal. At times you might even feel as if it would be easier to return to your unhealthy eating habits. But keep in mind, with each passing day you will grieve less and less over the loss of your addiction. It may occasionally reach for you, but the key is, don't reach back!

We read in our key verse that when Jacob finished instructing his sons, "he breathed his last, and was gathered to his people." Every professional embalmer knows that in order to make a good mummy, something has to die. I am sure you can start the process prematurely, but I have a feeling it would not go well for the candidate! The Greek word for death is *nekros*, and it means separation from God. But when you think about it, death is really separation from anything that makes us feel alive. We call it death when our bodies separate from our spirits. However, when you are separated from the life you truly want, you can feel dead—dead to your dreams, ambitions, and goals.

Physical death doesn't mean nonexistence because there is no such thing as nonexistence. Death just means your body and your spirit have separated. In life, we often feel "dead" when we are separated from the purpose for which our hearts ache. In my counseling office I often hear people say, "Larry, I just feel dead on the inside." This just goes to show, *you don't have to die to be dead!*

Usually when people feel dead, it's because they have an unfulfilled ache in their hearts. Most of the time it is connected to something they feel needs to change.

In order for the new to come, the old has to die. Jesus said, "Unless a grain of wheat is buried in the ground, dead to the world, it is never any more than a grain of wheat. But if it is buried, it sprouts and reproduces itself many times over" (John 12:24, THE MESSAGE).

If you want the new, don't be afraid to submit to the embalming process. Expect to grieve the loss of whatever had you bound for so long, but don't park there. Release the old, dead things of your past and reach toward the new life you desire.

REFLECTION JOURNAL

How will you prepare yourself for the withdrawal of leaving the old behind?

_____

_____

_____

_____

_____

_____

_____

_____

_____

_____

_____

_____

_____

_____

Part XII

The Most Dangerous Place Is "Almost There"

But when they came to Harran, they settled there.
—Genesis 11:31

Ten years from now, make sure you can say that
you chose your life; you didn't settle for it.[1]
—Mandy Hale

Day 38

DON'T DIE IN HARRAN

Today consider all the times you have settled
for "good enough" rather than pushing on
to "best." You're too close to give up now!

Key Verse: *But when they came to
Harran, they settled there.*
—GENESIS 11:31

Now THAT YOU are hungry for change and have
decided to reach for the future you know God has in
store for you, it will be easy to settle for "almost there." You
have to make up your mind not to die in Harran.

> Terah took his son Abram and his grandson Lot, son of
> Haran, and his daughter-in-law Sarai, his son Abram's
> wife, and they went out together from Ur of the Chaldeans
> to go into the land of Canaan; but when they came to
> Harran, they settled there. The days of Terah were two
> hundred and five years, and Terah died in Harran.
> —GENESIS 11:31–32

These are sobering verses of Scripture. Abram's father,
Terah, decided it was time for change. He decided that it
was time to go to the Promised Land, but when they got to
Harran, the Bible says, "They settled there." Not only did
they settle there, Terah died there! Wow! Terah heard the
call, took the deal, read this book, and started toward his

future, but somewhere along the way he settled, just like you and I have done so many times.

He was headed to Canaan, the land flowing with milk and honey, but at some point on his journey for change, he found an OK city and settled there.

You may have started your journey to Canaan a thousand times before and each time you reached an OK place and stopped there. Instead of pushing on to what you really wanted, you settled for the mediocre. Any time you get to that mediocre place in life, you must make a decision: Do I settle here and die, or do I confront myself and push on?

The most dangerous place in life is "almost there." When you're "almost there," you will be tempted to settle for second best. At this point in your forty-day journey, you may be terrified of day 41. You may be worn out from confronting yourself and your past, and you may feel as if you're in an OK place, so you will just stop. You may think, "I am tired of suffering through these cravings, I am tired of all this healthy living and exercise, and I am tired of being sweet to my enemies."

You may be getting sick of keeping your commitments, doing the hard work, and depriving your flesh of whatever it's still screaming for. But please don't settle in Harran when Canaan is just around the corner! You can do this! Don't die in the land of OK. Press on to the land of extraordinary. When facing change, let perspective, not circumstances, be your compass.

Life is all about perspective. Terah clearly lost his somewhere along the way. This stands in stark contrast to the men we've already discussed in previous days. Jesus and David refused to allow their circumstances to affect their perspectives. When Jesus faced His forty days in the wilderness with the Devil, He was guided by the right perspective. He would not be distracted by His friends, enemies, family, circumstances, or His flesh. He kept moving in the right direction despite the opposition.

In life your circumstances will rarely be cheering for you as you make the changes necessary to reach your potential. In order to successfully complete this journey, the right perspective must be your compass.

A lot of people have what I call a *Hee Haw* perspective. Depending upon your age, you may or may not remember the television show *Hee Haw*. For those of you who may be too young to remember, the show was kind of like *Saturday Night Live* for hillbillies! I can say that because I was raised in the Ozarks. There was this reoccurring skit that featured a bunch of down-on-their luck hillbilly folk singing a song about gloom, despair, agony, depression, and misery. The singers confessed that if they didn't have bad luck, they would have no luck at all. Unfortunately that is the theme song for those of us who allow our negative circumstances to lead the way.

In life there are really only two compasses. The first compass is our circumstances, and for many of us this compass gets to decide most everything. However, following the compass of circumstances will always cause us to lose our way. The second compass is perspective, and with the right perspective we can stay on course even when our opposition shows up on a regular basis. To be successful, you cannot live a circumstance-based life. You must live a perspective-based life. It is the only way to lasting change.

On the way to Canaan, Terah settled. We are not given many details about why he did so or the circumstances surrounding that decision, but it is clear that he lost his perspective. To make matters worse, he ended up dying there. He would be buried in the land where he settled.

Don't be like Terah. Don't settle for second best. Don't die in Harran.

REFLECTION JOURNAL

Consider the times in your life when you stopped just short of your goal. How will you push on this time when you find yourself almost there?

_____

_____

_____

_____

_____

_____

_____

_____

_____

_____

_____

Day 39

WHO INVITED YOU?

I would say you still have at least one
hitchhiker—a familiar behavior that is saying
to you, "How can you leave me behind? After
all, we are family!" Don't be fooled.

Key Verse: *So Abram departed, as the LORD had
spoken to him, and Lot went with him. Abram was
seventy-five years old when he departed from Harran.*
—GENESIS 12:4

WHEN ABRAM SET out to find his future, he picked up
a hitchhiker. His nephew Lot decided to come along
for the journey. Sadly Lot's patterns and predictable behaviors would prove fatal.

In life you will pick up many uninvited hitchhikers, and
like Lot, most of them won't have anything to contribute.
Lot was a hindrance. Like an albatross around Abram's
neck, he would only make a difficult trip more difficult.
Nonetheless, Abram seemed to tolerate his presence, at
least at first. Lot was raised to keep covenant with Jehovah,
but in time he would be swayed by the seductive call of
Sodom and Gomorrah.

Any time you start toward your future, "Lot" will be
standing at your door, bags packed! Lot always wants to
tag along. The differences between Abram and Lot are not
hard to identify. Abram was instructed by God and had
fully committed himself to the journey before him. Lot, on

the other hand, wanted to impose himself into God's plan without the call or commitment required.

By now you are reaching the end your forty-day challenge. As you begin to think about day 41, be prepared for Lot to invite himself along. You are not the only one excited about the journey. Those old habits, patterns, and predictable behaviors from your past are not going to allow you to leave them behind without some protest. Just as it was with Abram, there will be opposition in pursuit.

When Abram left for Canaan, in obedience to the Lord, the Bible says Lot went with him. In this story there is no mention of God telling Abram to take his nephew. Lot apparently took it upon himself to tag along with Uncle Abram. We would later find out why God did not request Lot's presence on this trip. Lot was trouble. From his hard-to-get-along-with herdsmen to his love affair with Sodom, Lot was constantly causing problems. As he and Abram traveled together, it would soon become obvious that if Abram wanted the life God had arranged, he would need to separate from his half-delivered nephew.

This is a picture of our lives. As we set out for the future we want, we must uninvite the uninvited. Like the crazy uncle who shows up once a year and ruins the family reunion, Lot will always be looking to crash your party! Abram could have said, "If Lot is going, then I am not going." Or Abram could have waited for Lot to somehow magically disappear before he began the trip. This is often the case with us. We know where we want to go, but we also know who will be tagging along, so we just decide not to go at all. We never reach the future we want because we are unwilling to even start moving toward it.

At some point you have to say, "Lot, get in the car!" Or, "Insecurity, get in the car!" Or, "Unhealthy habits get in the car!" Or, "Trauma from my past, get in the car!" But you must say to those things, "If you insist on coming, then you will come on my terms!" Lot had been a part of Abram's life for many years. Abram was well-versed in his nephew's ways, yet Abram allowed him to tag along even though he knew Lot would make the journey a struggle.

Hebrews 12:1 tells us to throw off everything that hinders us and the sin that so easily entangles so we can run with perseverance. There is a big difference between getting rid of sin and getting rid of yourself. Your old patterns and predictable behaviors have no doubt engrained themselves into your everyday life. You may not be able to throw them off at first. But think about this: you have spent the last thirty-nine days confronting the way you have allowed yourself to become. Even if Lot has been tagging along, don't forfeit all the time you've invested. Keep moving forward.

In Genesis 13:5–11 we read that Lot and Abram had to separate because they both had flocks, herds, and tents, and the land couldn't support them both. Just as Abram had to part with Lot in order to move forward, eventually you too will need to part with your familiar bad habits, old patterns, and destructive behaviors. After you have faced your devils for forty days, you must part with them for good! If they go to the left, you go to the right. If they go to the right, you go to the left. Abram made it clear, if

Lot went one way, he was going the other. He would not risk the two of them crossing paths.

Why? The land simply could not support both of them. Only after Lot departed was Abram able to move into another level of living. Lot moved into Sodom, a place that would come to be known for its wickedness, and Abram moved into Canaan, a land of blessing.

> After Lot had departed from him, the LORD said to Abram, "Lift up now your eyes, and look from the place where you are, northward and southward and eastward and westward. All the land that you see I will give to you and to your descendants forever."
>
> —GENESIS 13:14–15

After your forty-day challenge is complete, you will be faced with day 41. For weeks you have been doing the right thing, and I hope you have learned to let go of whatever you identified as your reason for beginning this book. So now what?

The next step is to lift your eyes and see the future. No matter which direction Abram looked, he could see the future. The future was before him, behind him, and on both sides. Once Lot was subtracted from the equation, the doors of opportunity and freedom were thrown open. Abram eventually realized he would never get to Canaan until he parted company with everything holding him back. Separation would be essential.

Starting this forty-day journey is the first step, even if you have to leave with Lot tagging along. But the second step is letting Lot go. God tolerated Lot for a time as he traveled with Abram, but it became evident that at some point he had to be turned loose. God is patient. He knows when you begin this journey, more than likely Lot will still be with you. But as you move closer and closer toward Canaan, Lot must slowly be removed.

> Now Lot, who was moving about with Abram...
> —GENESIS 13:5, NIV

Lot was perfectly content to spoil the journey, so Abram had to make the decision to turn him loose. Lot would not go on his own accord. In much the same way at some point you must say, "Lot, it's time for you to leave."

Don't get sentimental with your devils. Lot was familiar. Lot was comfortable. Lot was even loved. He was, after all, family. The little boy who had no doubt played in the floor of Uncle Abe's tent had to be removed. Your old patterns of failure are a lot like Lot. They can become as familiar and comforting as a nephew playing in the sand just outside your front door. Don't get sentimental with your devils.

After your forty-day challenge is completed, the familiar will always try to return. Like the children of Israel who left slavery but still pined for the pots of meat they left behind in Egypt, you will be tempted to return to the comfortable. Slavery was terrible, but the children of Israel were used to it, and there were no surprises. To be successful beyond this forty-day challenge, you need a new comfortable.

The old comfortable needs to make you uncomfortable! It's always easier to do what we have always done. The problem with that is, if you do what you have always done, you will reap what you have always had. To get what you've never had, you must do what you've never done.

It's easy to get sentimental with our past and just accept certain things as if we have no power to change them. Abram could have limped through life carrying Lot; instead he let him go. You must do the same.

REFLECTION JOURNAL

Are you willing to tell Lot that he is not invited? Consider the hitchhikers from your past that have found a way into your future. What will you do to separate yourself from them?

_____

_____

_____

_____

_____

_____

_____

_____

_____

_____

_____

_____

_____

Day 40

REFUSE TO RESCUE LOT

Congratulations, you made it! The last thirty-nine days have, no doubt, at times felt like a roller-coaster ride. The important thing is that you continued to make progress. Today use your time to focus on why Lot should be left with the enemy.

Key Verse: *He recovered all the goods and brought back his relative Lot and his possessions, together with the women and the other people.*
—GENESIS 14:16, NIV

AFTER ABRAM AND Lot separated, Lot found his residence in Sodom and Gomorrah, cities where the people sinned greatly against the Lord (Gen. 13:13).

It was a godless society. Before its destruction, the Lord could not even find ten righteous people living there. It was full of pride, homosexuality, and rebellion against God. This was not a fitting place for a relative of Abram's. Yet Lot and his family seemed to assimilate quickly.

Soon after Lot's arrival, Sodom was attacked by four enemy kings. The battle was lost, and Lot was taken as a prisoner.

Then they took all the possessions of Sodom and Gomorrah, and all their provisions, and departed. They also took Lot, Abram's brother's son, who lived in Sodom, and his possessions, and went their way.
—GENESIS 14:11–12

Upon hearing about the capture of his nephew, Abram devised a rescue plan.

> When Abram heard that his relative was taken captive, he armed his three hundred and eighteen trained servants born in his own house, and pursued them as far as Dan. During the night he divided his men to attack them and defeated them, and pursued them as far as Hobah, which is north of Damascus. He brought back all the possessions, along with his relative Lot and his possessions, and also the women and the people.
>
> —Genesis 14:14–16

After your forty-day challenge is over, you are going to be tempted to bring back that destructive behavior you worked so hard to get rid of. Keep in mind, Lot had not changed since his departure. If he was allowed back into Abram's camp, the results would be a disaster. Your old patterns may be familiar, and you might even miss them from time to time. They have been a part of your life for so long it would be easy for you to devise a plan to rescue them. But remember, those behaviors, like Lot, haven't changed. The misery they brought you before, they will bring to you again.

Lot would eventually leave Abram again and go right back to Sodom, but the city would again be in crisis. This time God Himself would rain down fire and brimstone to level Sodom and Gomorrah. Not even Abram, with all his pleading, could convince God otherwise. In fact, the Bible makes a point of stating that the fire and brimstone

"was from the Lord out of heaven" and that God "over-
threw those cities, all the valley, all the inhabitants of the
cities, and what grew on the ground" (Gen. 19:24–25).
Considering how wicked these cities must have been, Lot's
return to Sodom only confirms how important it was for
him to be separated from Abram.

With Lot in the camp, Abram's future would always be
at risk. The ungrateful nephew not only complicated the
present, he would have also destroyed the future. It was
Abram's willingness to finally cut ties with Lot that con-
tributed to his new, prosperous life in Canaan.

*Get rid of your Lots, even if it hurts. Your future depends
on it.*

Many of the heroes outlined in this book were not heroes
at all. They, like you, were just regular people, leading
regular lives. They were raising families, getting married,
moving to new cities, working ordinary jobs, and doing
battle with the desires of their flesh.

The difference, however, was their willingness to face
their personal devils—from Moses, who committed
murder, to David, who committed adultery, to Abraham,
who could not seem to tell the truth, to Jonah, who chroni-
cally whined. They weren't superhuman; they were simply
willing to confront the ridiculous behavior that kept them
trapped in a second-best life.

Forty days spent confronting your devils can lead to the
life you have been looking for. We see this perfectly illus-
trated in the life of Jesus. We started in Luke chapter 4. It
seems only fitting that we should end there as well.

After Jesus spent forty days in the wilderness with the Devil, everything changed. Suddenly we start reading stories about Jesus casting demons out of people, healing the sick, raising the dead, and bending the very laws of nature. His forty days with the Devil prepared Him for the future God had planned for Him.

Obviously His time with the Devil was well spent. It positioned Jesus for success. His level of influence was elevated in both the physical and spiritual realms. People marveled at His teaching and wondered what manner of man He was. He turned a ragtag bunch of fishermen into world changers. If Jesus had skipped this very important step, His future would have been at risk. Your future is also at risk.

Your forty-day journey may be coming to an end, but there is still a challenge before you. Your Lot—those old, familiar habits—will want to tag along with you as you move into your future. Refuse to let them hitchhike. You will be tempted to settle in "almost there"; don't take the bait. Stay focused on the future God has for you; let the right perspective, not your desires or your circumstances, be your compass. Only then will you begin to live in your "Canaan," which is the dream life God put in your heart.

That life can be yours—I, along with many others, am a living witness—but only if you continue to refuse to stay the same.

REFLECTION JOURNAL

How will you safeguard yourself once Lot is gone? Use your journal time on this last day of the challenge to write out the destructive things that could happen if you were to "rescue Lot." When tempted to bring him back, don't forget the chaos and confusion that accompanies him. Leave Lot behind!

_____

_____

_____

_____

_____

_____

_____

_____

_____

_____

_____

_____

_____

_____

_____

_____

_____

CONCLUSION

*Therefore, if any man is in Christ, he is
a new creature. Old things have passed
away. Look, all things have become new.*

—2 CORINTHIANS 5:17

NOW THAT YOU have allowed the Holy Spirit to partner with you to change, your life will no longer be the same. Second Corinthians 5:17, written by a man who would describe himself as the chief of sinners, knew all too well that change is deliberate. Yes, Paul would have a salvation experience on the road to Damascus, but his eventual transformation into a new creation was in part due to the fact that he decided to change. Saul of Tarsus became Paul the Apostle. The old would go and the new would come.

You have spent the last forty days becoming the person that God created you to be. It's nice to finally meet you!

You are a new creation! The fat kid in the mirror went on to become a marathon runner. The pastor being tempted to throw away his family and career went on to become a man who not only overcame his struggles but also showed others how to do the same. My identity has always hinged on my willingness to show up in the wilderness and face my devils. Such is the case with you!

My name is Larry Dugger. I spent forty days with the Devil, and the Devil didn't make it!

NOTES

PART I—THE DEVIL WANTS YOU TO TRADE GROWTH FOR GRATIFICATION

1. BrainyQuote.com, "Rod Parsley Quotes," accessed January 12, 2016, http://www.brainyquote.com/quotes /quotes/r/rodparsley504983.html.

PART II—PROGRESS IS MORE IMPORTANT THAN PERFECTION

1. Leo Tolstoy, *Anna Karenina*, trans. Constance Garnett (New York: P. F. Collier & Son, 1917).

PART IV—IT'S JUST THE USUAL

1. Searchquotes.com, "Sir Patrick Moore Quotes," accessed February 17, 2016, http://www.searchquotes .com/search/Sir_Patrick_Moore/.

PART V—DEFIANCE ON A DAILY BASIS

1. As quoted in Aldric Marshall, *Success Behind the Scars* (Mustang, OK: Tate Publishing & Enterprises, LLC, 2008), 179.

PART VI—MISSION: IMPOSSIBLE

1. BrainyQuote.com, "Robert H. Schuller Quotes," accessed January 15, 2016, http://www.brainyquote .com/quotes/quotes/r/roberthsc121269.html.

PART VII—DON'T JUST DREAM
WHILE YOU ARE ASLEEP

1.   BrainyQuote.com, "Colin Powell Quotes," accessed
     January 20, 2016, http://www.brainyquote.com/quotes
     /quotes/c/colinpowel385927.html.

DAY 25—A DREAM WITHOUT A
PLAN IS A NIGHTMARE

1.   Wikipedia.org, "John 'Hannibal' Smith," accessed Jan-
     uary 22, 2016, https://en.wikipedia.org/wiki/John
     _%22Hannibal%22_Smith.

DAY 31—YOU CAN'T HANDLE THE TRUTH

1.   *A Few Good Men*, directed by Rob Reiner (Culver City,
     CA: Sony Pictures Home Entertainment, 2001), DVD.

PART X—CHANGE IS POSSIBLE WHEN
YOU HAVE HAD ENOUGH

1.   BrainyQuote.com, "Lao Tzu Quotes," accessed January
     23, 2016, http://www.brainyquote.com/quotes/quotes
     /l/laotzu121075.html.

2.   John C. Maxwell, *Leadership Principles for Graduates*
     (Nashville: Thomas Nelson, 2007).

PART XII—THE MOST DANGEROUS
PLACE IS "ALMOST THERE"

1.   Goodreads.com, "Mandy Hale Quotes," accessed Jan-
     uary 23, 2016, http://www.goodreads.com/quotes
     /862055-ten-years-from-now-make-sure-you-can-say
     -that.

For more information about Larry Dugger, visit his website at LarryDugger.com.

You can also follow him at:
Twitter/LarryDugger40
Facebook.com/LarryDugger

To get in touch with Larry or to book a speaking engagement, contact him at:

dugg@fidnet.com

417-650-8841

P. O. Box 1848
Lebanon, MO 65536

CONNECT WITH US!

CHARISMA HOUSE

(Spiritual Growth)

Facebook.com/CharismaHouse

@CharismaHouse

Instagram.com/CharismaHouseBooks

(Health)

Pinterest.com/CharismaHouse

REALMS

(Fiction)

Facebook.com/RealmsFiction